WORLD OF CULTURE

ARCHITECTURE

by David Jacobs

Newsweek Books, New York

*Grateful acknowledgment is made for the use of excerpted material on pages
154–179 from the following works:*
An Autobiography by Frank Lloyd Wright. Copyright © 1932 by Frank Lloyd
Wright. All rights reserved. Reprinted by permission of Mrs. Frank Lloyd Wright.
Beyond Habitat by Moshe Safdie. Copyright © 1970 by Moshe Safdie. Reprinted
by permission of Mr. Safdie and MIT Press.
Eero Saarinen on His Work. Edited by Aline B. Saarinen. Revised edited copy-
right © 1968 by Yale University. By permission of Yale University Press.
"Form and Design," an address by Louis I. Kahn. By permission of Louis I. Kahn.
"Unity in Diversity" by Walter Gropius from *Four Great Makers of Modern
Architecture.* Copyright © 1963 by Trustees of Columbia University. By per-
mission of De Capo Press and the School of Architecture, Columbia University.
Frank Lloyd Wright: Writings and Buildings, edited by Edgar Kaufmann and
Ben Raeburn, copyright 1960, by permission of Horizon Press, New York.
"The Tall Building Artistically Considered" from *Kindergarten Chats and Other
Writings* by Louis H. Sullivan. Copyright © 1947 by Wittenborn, Schultz, Inc.
Reprinted by permission of the publisher, Wittenborn, Schultz, Inc.
The Ludwig Mies van der Rohe address to the Illinois Institute of Technology is
from *Mies van der Rohe* by Philip C. Johnson, second edition revised. Copyright
1947, 1953 by The Museum of Modern Art, New York. All rights reserved. Re-
printed by permission of the publisher, and with the courtesy of the Mies van
der Rohe Archive of The Museum of Modern Art.
Nine Chains to the Moon by R. Buckminster Fuller. Copyright © 1938, 1963 by
R. Buckminster Fuller. Reprinted by permission of Doubleday & Company, Inc.
The Spaces In Between by Nathaniel A. Owings. Copyright © 1973 by Nathaniel
A. Owings. Reprinted by permission of Houghton Mifflin Company.
"The Seven Crutches of Architecture" by Philip C. Johnson from *Perspecta 3.*
Reprinted by permission of Philip C. Johnson.
Towards a New Architecture by Le Corbusier. Copyright © 1927 by Fondation
Le Corbusier. Reprinted by permission of Helena Strassova.

ISBN: Regular edition 0-88225-107-4 ISBN: Deluxe edition 0-88225-108-2
Library of Congress Catalog Card No. 73-89394
© 1974 Europa Verlag. All rights reserved.
Printed and bound by Mondadori, Verona, Italy.

Contents

1

Who's in Charge Here?

THE STORY OF BUILDING starts with a familiar ring, for it starts the way stories of so many of mankind's enterprises start—speculatively and in the almost immeasurably distant past.

The glaciers were receding toward the earth's poles, and game animals were following the melting ice. As his once-plentiful prey dwindled in number, man the hunter went down from the mountains to the plains and river valleys and became man the farmer. Because there were no caves in the lowlands, he had to think of ways to shelter himself and his family. He looked around, examined the materials available to him, tried this and that, and made something. Sometimes he formed a circle with reeds forced upright into the ground, arched the stalks inward, binding them together at the top, and covered the frame with papyrus. Other times he made a skeletal cone with sticks and gave it a cover of skins. In one place he heaped rocks to form a hollow hemisphere; in another place he shaped a square-walled hut of mud and roofed it with grass or leaves; elsewhere he gathered fallen branches for a timber hut and used bark or brush for the roof. Ingenious man had made a home; man the builder had arrived.

Primeval man's solutions to the problems of devising shelter were indeed ingenious, but they were not necessarily evidence of the superior intellect that was making him master of his world. *Homo sapiens* was not the only living creature with the sense to come in out of the rain. He was by no means alone in his ability to manufacture a place of refuge; and neither his constructive use of native materials, nor the complexity of his structural systems was unique. For the making of shelters was instinctive in man, as it was and is in countless other species. And if the tent and mud or timber hut seem remarkably sophisticated to have been products of mere animal instinct, they certainly were no more sophisticated than the bee's hive, the ant's labyrinth, the oriole's nest, or the beaver's dam.

The need for shelter probably had less significance than is usually supposed in the long evolutionary process that ultimately produced architecture. These earliest structures were, of course, enormously important; the act of building, after all, had to be learned before the art of building could appear. Moreover, as soon as these dwellings were completed their builders assigned to them a host of magical and mystical properties, and this spiritualism (which was unique to *Homo sapi-*

Today only ruins remain, but the structures known as nuraghe (left), erected by Bronze-Age inhabitants of Sardinia, show a sophisticated grasp of how to build in stone. The complexes consisted of huge, hollow, central cones surrounded by massive walls dotted with round towers. Walls and towers alike were honeycombed with passageways and chambers.

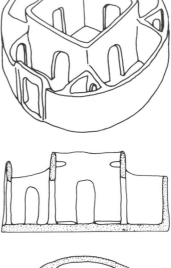

ens) evolved apace with building skills. But the fact that structures were shelters—the humans' equivalent of the nest—does not seem to have mattered very much.

To verify this contention one need only take a cursory look at the evolution of ordinary dwellings and try to relate it to the evolution of the world's major architecture. It can be an exasperating experience to try to trace, step by step, the way huts and lean-tos developed into pyramids and Greek and Roman temples. But separate the two evolutions and the picture is clearer—chiefly because there really are two separate developments. Now it is easy to see how the primitive sacrificial altar evolved into the Greek temple, which became the Roman basilica, which evolved into the Byzantine palace in the East and into the Romanesque monastery in the West, and how the great Gothic cathedrals evolved from both the Byzantine and Romanesque structures. Now it is also apparent that ordinary dwellings evolved very differently, very slowly, that the mud hut took a thousand years to evolve into a slightly larger mud hut and another thousand to evolve into a mud hut with three rooms instead of one, and then two thousand more years to evolve into a six-room adobe cottage.

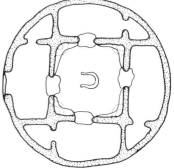

Architecture is related to mankind's need for shelter in one way, though—to the same extent that painting is related to mankind's need for food. Even while he was still up in the icy mountains, early man was flexing his intellectual muscles, doing things the lower animals could not do and then trying to figure out why he had done them. At one point he found he could make a likeness of the game he hunted. When he saw the likeness on the cave wall he believed it magical—perhaps he had captured the soul of the animal in the likeness, and if its soul were in his possession, he would have an easier time than usual capturing its body. Buoyed by this belief, the confident hunter may well

The Belgian flintstone cave at left was used as a dwelling by Neolithic man during the third millennium B.C. At the same time, his counterparts in Mesopotamia were already developing the far more advanced structure shown above (from top to bottom) in reconstruction, elevation, and floor plan. Much later, and motivated by reasons of religion rather than shelter, the unknown people who inhabited Britain erected their famous monument at Stonehenge (right).

have had an unusually successful hunt the next time out. The value of the pictures was thus proven, and the practice of making such depictions spread, giving birth to both painting and writing. Eventually the specific connection between the pictures and the need for food disappeared, but the spiritual relationship that exists between painting and man has remained.

So it was with building. The need for shelter produced the first building, but once the dwelling existed it was called a magic place. In order to acknowledge its spiritual powers people developed elaborate rituals: in a one-family hut the adult males sat in a certain place, facing in a proscribed direction, perhaps in a specified posture; the women had their rules and directions; so did the children. When communal dwellings appeared, the arrangements were even more elaborate. And of course when highly civilized man builds a building, he follows the same old habits: at the conference table or in parliament, the seating arrangements are labored over and clearly defined; even in a suburban home it is not unusual for each member of the family to take the same seat at the breakfast table each morning.

The special, spiritual relationship that exists between people and building—between, for that matter, people and just about everything that people purposefully create—existed from the time when people started making things. When architecture finally did materialize, that relationship was enlarged and embellished. But that relationship did not

For all their highly developed society, the nomadic Plains Indians of North America could not be called fully civilized; living in buffalo-hide tepees (left), they had no permanent architecture. In contrast, the Incas of South America built vast, monumental stone cities such as Machu Picchu (right) thus qualifying for a place on the roster of the civilized peoples of the world.

Overleaf: *The Temple of the Warriors at Chichén Itzá shows the grandeur as well as the obvious technical expertise of Mesoamerican architects. Its Toltec influence is made manifest by the widespread use of columns. Toltec builders used columns and beams to support slab roofs far larger than anything the Maya could construct using their corbelled arch.*

create architecture. For its real genesis, architecture required more than people; it required more than groups of people. It required highly organized, large groups of people—it required civilization.

Architecture is a badge of civilization. According to prevailing historical viewpoints in recent centuries, it is the requisite sign, the certain credential without which a society cannot be called civilized. The vaguely known and dimly differentiated nomads who crossed the steppes of Eurasia, overran the crumbling Roman Empire, and settled Western Europe had languages and laws, a social structure that had evolved over centuries, some political institutions, and a long artistic tradition. What they did not have was architecture. Thus they were barbarians, and barbarians they remained until they learned to build with stone. (It took them two centuries, a period known as the Dark Ages.) When they did learn, they officially stopped being barbarians and started being Europeans. In contrast, societies with less structure, few institutions, and even backward technology are likely to be given the benefit of the doubt—and official certification—if they created an architecture. The Maya had no wheel, and the Incas had no written language, but both cultures produced great architectural complexes, and therefore both are entitled to be called civilizations.

Architecture is a reasonable measure for the existence of civilization because it proclaims, as few other products of a society proclaim, that

the society expects to survive, progress, and prosper beyond the present, that it intends to outlive all of its current members. The Franks, Huns, Goths, Normans, and many of the others we lump together under the barbarian standard were excellent craftsmen. They made fine weaponry, utensils, and garments with care and a real aesthetic sense; their decorative patterns had been handed down and refined for scores of generations. But however fine their art, it was a portable art; where was their monumental art? It didn't exist, for these premedieval settlers had only recently been nomads, and nomads do not build monuments because tomorrow they will be on their way.

Compare the nomads with the Romans, who no sooner conquered a land than they built a monument on it—a triumphal arch, or perhaps a whole Roman city to celebrate not merely military triumph but the dominance and immortality of Roman civilization. It is no accident that Roman ruins still stand in England, across France into Italy and through Greece and Turkey, along the African shores of the Mediterranean Sea, in Syria, in Palestine, in Egypt. The Romans took themselves seriously, and their architecture symbolized their confidence that Rome would prevail forever.

Architecture not only proclaims the existence of a civilization; it is a cultural phenomenon that reveals information about the society that built it with unequivocal directness. Unlike painting, sculpture, literature, the dramatic arts, theology, politics, and historical discourse, architecture almost never minces words. The arts, letters, philosophies, and recorded histories of a society may and do reveal the sense of values—aspirations and ideals, weaknesses and follies—that prevailed in that society, or reflect or interpret the events that occurred. Architecture deals in more basic information. It comes right to the point and tells us what we ought to know before we can begin to understand the ideas and events. It defines, most significantly, the main source of power in the society; and it also explains what the central cultural concern of the society was.

14

Succeeding generations and succeeding cultures have always borrowed what they wanted from their predecessors, as is shown here in the development of religious architecture. From the classic simplicity of the Greek temple at Agrigento (far left) evolved the Roman Basilica of Maxentius (the present ruins shown at left with a reconstruction in cross section below it), the Byzantine Monastery of St. Theodore (above), the Romanesque Cathedral of Modena (right), and the soaring majesty that is the hallmark of Gothic church building (far right).

Fifteenth-century Florence has been proclaimed—and proclaimed itself—the heart of a great new age, characterized by the spirit of humanism. From there on in the welfare of people—ordinary people—was to be a chief concern of society. The humanist literature of the ancient Greeks and Romans was revived; scholars dipped deep into Plato and Aristotle in an effort to reconsider and redefine the ethics that guided the affairs of men; sculptors celebrated the beauty of the human body; and painters depicted the saints in homely terms so that all would know that the holiest souls and the simplest folk were cast of the same flesh and blood. The arts and letters, then, boldly asserted that here was an age and a society with only the highest aspirations.

Now look at the architecture. In form it was Neoclassical, and that seemed to fit. But what were these new structures rising in Florence? They were primarily palaces and banking houses, but they were built like fortresses: no windows or only very tiny windows at the ground level; plenty of niches—nicely concealed behind floriate scrolls or other embellishments—for soldiers; central courts to provide for a breath of air without exposure to the rabble. Apparently there was a broad gap between aspirations and reality in Renaissance Florence; the arts other than architecture expressed the former, architecture the latter. It almost always does.

The fundamental question that the architecture of any culture answers is: who's in charge here? If we knew nothing whatever about Western history except the information revealed by its architecture, we would know a great deal. Without too much trouble we could discern that Egypt was an extremely rigid society, incredibly slow to change, and ruled by a powerful authority who was thought to be a deity. We would be able to trace the rise of the Church as the prevailing power in medieval Europe; and if we looked carefully enough we could also see—contained in the very cathedrals that proclaimed the power of the Church—evidence of the decline of the Church's power and of the rise of secularism.

The seventeenth and eighteenth centuries are defined conspicuously, at times ostentatiously, through architecture as an age of kings and courtiers. Entering the epoch of the republican revolutions we can look for signs that at last the people had become the ones in charge–and find fewer indications than we might have expected. And in our own time we can keep the inquiry alive: who's in charge here, we ask, and for an answer name the names of the most notable ten or fifteen buildings of the present generation. They would include Lever Brothers, Seagram, CBS, Ford Foundation in New York; John Hancock in Chicago; Transamerica in San Francisco. Sometimes architecture gives up its information readily, sometimes it is more enigmatic; but the information is always there. To seek out and reveal this information is one of the primary purposes of this book.

In addition to supplying basic information about individual cultures, the history of architecture, viewed overall, provides a picture of the continuous processes that have shaped the history of civilization. For architecture has evolved very smoothly; its history has a greater continuity than that of the other arts. There are two main reasons for this continuity: one is function, and the other is cost.

Architecture is, of course, an art, but it is also an eminently useful, practical science. As opposed to sculpture, which occupies space, architecture encloses space; and in a practical sense it is the enclosed space, the volume, that is of primary importance. In other words, it is not the walls that make a building useful, but rather the space enclosed and defined by the walls. The creative process of the architect is always circumscribed by the requirements of the space volume. If he is designing a palace, the architect must begin by calculating the number and size of the rooms required by the patron. Such specifications do not change very radically, even though the demands of the patrons may. One day the architect may be called upon to design a throne room, meeting rooms, and apartments for the monarch; another day he may be commissioned to design a building with a presidential office, cabinet meeting rooms, and apartments for the chief executive; but he is still working with similar specifications. The best he can do to reflect changing attitudes is to change the decor.

Architecture is not only functional; it is expensive. In all of the arts the artist is affected by the tastes of his patrons, and in all of the arts the artist functions as an influential tastemaker. Although the architect is no exception, he has more limitations than the sculptor or the painter, and his influence must be exerted much more slowly. This has been especially true since the appearance of sculpture and the easel painting. Since the age of Raphael, painters have been able to satisfy their patrons and themselves at the same time. While giving their patrons the sort of work they wanted, the painters could also work in the studio, experimenting, making revolutions. Since the time of Rembrandt many great painters have worked primarily for themselves, and have used their completed paintings to demonstrate the value of their experiments. One of the most famous examples of this are the Impressionists, who worked to satisfy no patronage, and who resorted to having their own unofficial exhibition to display their revolutionary works. Needless

to say, their revolution eventually caught on, and all subsequent painting—and much subsequent patronage—was affected.

The architect has had no such opportunity, simply because buildings cost so much money. The best an architect can do to make waves in his profession is to make and display visionary models or drawings of revolutionary architecture, but models and drawings do not make revolutions. Indeed the only revolutions that have occurred in the history of architecture are those forced by technology; and even those have been introduced so gradually that "revolution" hardly seems an appropriate word. From ancient times until the nineteenth century there really had been only two overall architectural styles—or master styles—and virtually all other styles were either departures from one or combinations of both. Then the elevator was invented, just in time to lend itself to the perfect new architecture for an urban-industrial age, the skyscraper. And yet even when the skyscraper appeared it was cloaked with Classical, Gothic, or Eclectic decor, or topped with a Lombardian villa or Greek temple. Not until after World War II did the camouflage come off to stay and a truly new idiom take over. This process may be exasperating for the most visionary architects, but it has given architecture its historical continuity and its documentary value as a gauge of civilization.

Architecture, then, has had a conservative evolution; so has civilization. They grew up together, the art and the acculturation, one not only symbolizing the other but expressing it. It has been that way from the start.

2

Mountains in the River Valleys

TWO OF THE WORLD's first great civilizations grew up independently of each other, although not too far apart, and were probably aware of each other's existence fairly early along. The monumental art that they developed, which would become history's first major architectural form, was similar, and yet it served very different functions. The form was the pyramid, which at its genesis was probably little more than a man-made mountain.

The civilizations were those that developed in Mesopotamia and Egypt, and both were agrarian. All early agricultural societies were, not unreasonably, greatly concerned with the forces of nature. The heat of the sun, the rain, and the cycles of the seasons were the forces that guided their planting, made their food grow, dictated the time for harvest. Thus the forces of nature became the first gods. Since these forces clearly dwelled above, in the skies, the skies themselves became holy. When it became standard practice—and no one knows when this was—to erect a shrine specifically for the purpose of paying homage to the gods, it was perfectly natural for people to want to build their temples in the highest possible spot, in order to get as close as possible to the home of the gods.

Both Mesopotamia and Egypt were flat valleys, the former enclosed by the Tigris and Euphrates rivers, and the latter flanking the Nile. For all intents and purposes there were no high places, and so the populations of both valleys manufactured mountains in order to achieve the physical intimacy with the heavens that they hoped would facilitate spiritual intimacy. The Mesopotamians probably had the idea first. In any case the earliest surviving Mesopotamian pyramid, the White Temple ziggurat at Warka (the biblical Erech) was built sometime between 3200 and 2850 B.C., whereas the oldest known Egyptian pyramid, over the tomb of King Zoser at Sakkara, is dated around 2778 B.C. The dates, however, are not as important as the fact that almost immediately after their respective appearances, the Mesopotamian and Egyptian pyramids assumed very different meanings. This should not be surprising, inasmuch as the societies themselves developed so differently.

Even though both the Mesopotamians and Egyptians were farmers dwelling in river valleys, their environmental circumstances were not the same. Egypt's valley was isolated—surrounded by the Mediterranean in the north and vast deserts everywhere else—and therefore secure.

Capped originally by a temple reached by ramps, the great ziggurat of Ur (left) is built on a solid core of sun-dried bricks. The true ziggurat, of which this is one, began to appear in the Tigris-Euphrates Valley as early as the fourth millennium B.C.

As families became communities and communities societies, it was easy for a coalescence to occur, for strong leaders to emerge, and for power to be solidified within, without fear of invasion from abroad. This internal, physical security surely accounts for the incredible continuity that characterized Egyptian civilization. Mesopotamia, in contrast, had no natural defenses. It was a fertile but marshy valley easily accessible from the lands around it—lands that were, if not entirely hospitable to emerging agrarian peoples, nonetheless traversable. The history of the region reflects the inconstancy of life in the Tigris-Euphrates valley, for there were no "Mesopotamians" as such, but rather a succession of distinct peoples who invaded or infiltrated. Usually they descended from the north, overcame by force or absorption the people who were there already, and instituted their own brands of civilization.

First were the admirable Sumerians, a people of vague origins, who probably wandered into Mesopotamia around 4000 B.C. Inventors of one of the world's first written languages, the Sumerians established many of the traditions in government, art, science, and religion that would characterize all of the Mesopotamian civilizations. About a thousand years after the arrival of the Sumerians, who settled and built their city-states mostly in the south, Semitic nomads began settling in the north, where they too built city-states. By the middle of the third millennium there were two strong cultures in Mesopotamia, Sumer in the south and Akkad in the north. In 2360 B.C. they were united—culturally as well as politically—and became the heart of the world's first empire, which extended from the Mediterranean to the Persian Gulf. During the height of this imperial era the Sumerian capital was Ur, perhaps history's first really cosmopolitan city. When Amorite Semites began pouring into Mesopotamia in the twentieth century B.C., however, the Sumerian-Akkadian unity that had created a golden age broke down. The empire quickly disintegrated, and Ur was destroyed.

During the next hundred years the Amorites settled down, the city-states developed independently, and the young city of Babylon began to prosper. In 1830 B.C. the Babylonian era came to Mesopotamia; it peaked under Hammurabi between 1728 and 1686 B.C. A city of reportedly astonishing magnificence, Babylon gave the world an enlightened code of laws and the basis of a lasting system of mathematical calculation. But Babylon, being Babylon, apparently had its mind on other matters when, around 1530 B.C., Hittite forces attacked the city, leveled it, and took everything of value from the rubble. They then went back to Asia Minor, leaving Mesopotamia leaderless and ripe for other invasions. The Kassites took advantage of the situation to seize power, but they made few cultural contributions during their centuries of ascendancy. Around 935 B.C. the Assyrians, who had been the dominant power in Upper Mesopotamia for four centuries, overpowered the whole valley and imposed their stern, warlike personality on the civilization. The Assyrians built an empire that transcended the Tigris and Euphrates, but in the sixth century B.C. it collapsed under a series of revolts. Soon thereafter the Persians arrived and essentially ended the three-thousand-year history of Mesopotamia's distinct and bounded civilization.

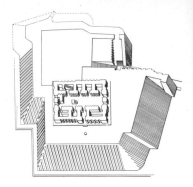

The reconstruction (above) of the White Temple of Warka shows the placement of that shrine on its ziggurat. At right is the great vaulted arch of the Palace of Khosrau at Ctesiphon.

Overleaf: This view of Persepolis shows the Apadana, or Throne Hall, of Xerxes—known as the Hall of a Hundred Columns—in the background. The Persians gloried in great square halls with a forest of columns supporting the high ceilings.

With that kind of history Mesopotamia could scarcely develop the political stability of Egypt. And yet, based on the evidence contained in three thousand years of architecture, there must have been a remarkable degree of consistency in Mesopotamian society—a much greater solidity than one might imagine for a culture so protean. Unfortunately, very little tangible evidence remains, although recently executed diagrammatic reconstructions of various examples of Mesopotamian architecture probably capture the spirit, if not the letter, of those massive ancient structures.

The reason why so few buildings have survived is simple: Mesopotamia was a land without wood and stone. The only building material available was mud; and although the Mesopotamians were quite inventive within their limitations, mud is hardly the sturdiest of materials. The Sumerians' White Temple—a whitewashed cubic shrine of mud— was placed upon a base of virtually solid clay modeled into a "mountain" with sloping sides, a flat top, and a long flight of stairs. As greater monumentality was desired in later structures, Sumerian builders sought a more flexible building module than raw clay and came up with the brick. Before long they realized that a baked brick was stronger and harder than a sun-dried brick. But the realization did not help them all that much, except academically; for the baking of bricks required the use of kilns, and the use of kilns required the existence of fuel, and the only fuel that burned hot enough to fire the bricks was— of course—wood, which had to be imported and was in short supply.

Sumerian builders and their successors did in fact oven-bake some bricks—the ones that would be placed at strategic points in important structures—but for the most part sun-dried brick had to suffice. It did for the moment, but not for posterity.

The ziggurat shape proved well suited to Mesopotamian cities for practical as well as spiritual reasons; and the cities tended to be built on elevated, receding terraces. Elevation was important because the region was largely swampland that often received weeks of rain at a time, followed by swarms of insects. By raising up the base, or street level of the cities, the Mesopotamians protected themselves from flood and plague. But there was another advantage to the elevated, three-dimensional cities; a terraced city with inclined ramps can grow vertically as well as horizontally, ensuring compactness and preventing sprawl. At the time of the Mesopotamians such designs also had the advantage of making the cities easy to defend, and there are architects and city planners today who wish that the Mesopotamian rather than the flat Greco-Roman model had been the one to influence Western architecture. (The contemporary visionary architect Paolo Soleri has named several of his designs for enormous, single-structure cities after Mesopotamian prototypes; Moshe Safdie and Buckminster Fuller have also acknowledged the superiority of the Mesopotamians' urban designs.)

The greatest of all Mesopotamian cities was Babylon. Actually, the city of which records exist—and which forms the basis for scholars' reconstructions—was not the capital city of Babylon's golden age, but the Babylon of Nebuchadnezzar II, who rebuilt it in the sixth century B.C. after the Assyrians had essentially destroyed the old city. How close the reconstructed city was to the original Babylon cannot be determined. Nevertheless, the new Babylon was a wonder of the ancient world.

Erected on the banks of the Euphrates, Babylon was enclosed by an enormous brick wall wide enough for a chariot drawn by four horses to make a U-turn on top. Within the wall were one hundred bronze gates, but the official entrance to the city was the north-facing Ishtar Gate, forty feet high and flanked by six towers. A reproduction of the Ishtar Gate has been built in Berlin, and it suggests some of the brilliance of the original—the animals carved in relief amid exquisitely colored glazed tiles, the beautiful decoration forming a frame, and the portal itself, a true arch. But the Berlin reconstruction could not possibly compare with what the Ishtar Gate must have looked like in Babylon, approached as it was by a broad avenue flanked by high walls on which were depicted in glazed-tile relief a procession of lions.

Inside the walls the city descended and rose in varying levels; planning was evident but zoning was not, and thus places of business and worship were juxtaposed with private dwellings, which were usually tiered. A long, broad processional way led to the high riverfront sites, where the buildings of greatest importance rose: the temple complex dedicated to Marduk, god of the city, dominated by the ziggurat that may have been the biblical Tower of Babel; the palaces; and that marvel of marvels, the Hanging Gardens of Babylon—a terraced monument on a site nine hundred by six hundred feet that rose in tiers to a

When Babylon was rebuilt fol
lowing its sack in 689 B.C. by
Sennacherib, it became the foremost city of the ancient world.
Strangers coming to it entered
by the Ishtar Gate, decorated
with dragons and bulls and approached by a processional way
(left) of awesome proportions.
All that remain are the ruined
walls (below). Sennacherib's father, Sargon II, built the city of
Khorsabad (right) containing
the earliest examples we have of
vaulted construction.

height of seventy-five feet. At each level was incredibly opulent foli-
age, much of it imported, and within, a maze of rooms radiated from a
huge throne room. Like the Ishtar Gate, the Hanging Gardens were
probably constructed by means of arches.

The arch was, it seems likely, developed first in Mesopotamia, and
its invention was responsible for one of the two main systems of building that have prevailed throughout history. One system is based on the
post and lintel—that is, vertical elements (posts) supporting, or holding
up, horizontal elements (lintels). The Egyptians employed the post-
and-lintel method for their buildings, using rows of cylindrical columns

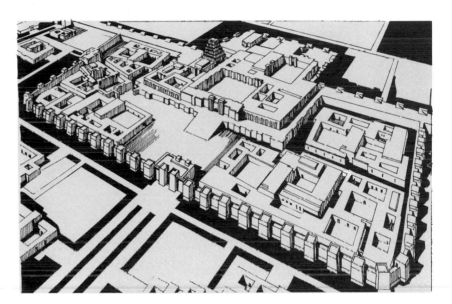

to support flat roofs. In post-and-lintel building, however, a reasonably
rigid element, usually either stone or timber, is required for the horizontal members. The Mesopotamians lacked both stone and timber; so
instead they built walls of incredible thickness and made structures that
were virtually solid, with "rooms" that were nothing more than the
spaces between the thicknesses. The Babylonians were among the first
to develop the corbeled, or false, arch to roof their rooms. A corbeled
arch is formed when each horizontal row of bricks at the top of a wall
is extended slightly beyond the row beneath it until, row by row, the
bricks close the space between walls and meet at the top row. The corbeled arch was suitable for portals, but prohibitive for roofing whole
rooms because the enclosure of a large space requires building an arch of
enormous height.

From the corbeled arch to the true arch would not seem to be such
an immense step, but it was. The corbeled arch had existed for centuries before anyone realized that a space between walls could be enclosed
by making wedge-shaped bricks (called voussoirs). By taking bricks
with beveled sides and placing them side-by-side one can make an arch
such as the one used at the Ishtar Gate. Continuous rows of wedge-
shaped bricks, or a continuous arch between two walls, makes a struc-

ture called a barrel vault, which is a suitable roofing form for a whole room. Some scholars believe that the Babylonians used the barrel vault, but there is no proof. However at Khorsabad, the capital city built by the eighth-century-B.C. Assyrian ruler Sargon II, the barrel vault was used extensively in the temple buildings. In any case, in the subsequent history of architecture, vaulted construction and post-and-lintel construction remained the two basic systems for building.

The Mesopotamian cities—of which Babylon was probably the supreme but not necessarily an atypical example—reflected the forces that guided the development of Mesopotamian civilization. Like the Egyptians, the peoples of the land between the rivers were religious. Their gods, personifications of natural phenomena, were earnestly revered, and no Mesopotamian city was complete without its grand ziggurat and a number of local chapels and temples to facilitate frequent daily worship. The earliest communities may in fact have been organized around the temples of priests who represented the patron deities. But because Mesopotamia was organized into city-states, the very necessities of governing stimulated the growth of a purely political establishment—something that did not materialize and was not needed in less urbanized, more centralized Egypt. Moreover, because Mesopotamia lacked so many essential natural resources, the civilizations that existed there were engraved in a lively foreign trade long before Egypt was. Commerce fostered the rise of an economically powerful and independent class of traders and other businessmen who were entitled to a say in the conduct of government.

As early as 280 B.C. Sumerian city-states were being ruled by a priest-king or a board of several priests along with an assembly of important citizens—a system part theocracy and part democracy. Indeed, commerce was so important to the Mesopotamians that the work of the priests, who were the first astrologers, botanists, mathematicians, and engineers, was often dedicated to the cause of extending commerce. And even as the primitive governments were replaced by powerful kings—who were sometimes deities, but more often simply divinely blessed mortals—the middle class remained extremely influential. To a significant extent the architecture of the Mesopotamian cities reflected its influence; there were dwellings for the most influential within the city walls, warehouses for exportable goods, and many large courts, particularly around the palace, where business was conducted. In sum, the Mesopotamian city was a prototype of the modern city, a cultural and commercial center; and if it was primarily a monument to king and gods, it also paid tribute to the economic and secular forces that were helping to shape the civilizations of the Tigris and Euphrates.

Egypt was a different story. For a substantial part of its history Egypt was almost purely agrarian. At the base of its culture was the village, not the city; and for a long time the society was relatively insular. The Nile valley, in which Egyptian civilization took shape, was only twelve miles at its widest point, although it extended along the riverbank for 950 miles. Herodotus described Egypt as "the gift of the Nile," and no wonder. The gentle, generous river seemed to give the Egyptians everything they needed in order to survive. Every July, the

The Step Pyramid of Zoser (right) was the first great edifice to be built of stone and remains one of the largest stone structures in the world. It is also the oldest building to record the name of its architect. Hieroglyphs spelling out Imhotep, the innovative genius who built it, are still existent.

Nile began its rise; every October it crested. When its innundation subsided it left a fresh supply of black alluvial soil—one of the richest and most fertile soils in the world—in the valley, and planting began. The Nile also made it easy for the earliest Egyptians to dig an elaborate network of irrigation canals to keep the soil fertile through the arid months. Finally the Nile was an easy means of communication and transportation in Egypt; it was the thoroughfare along which the country developed.

Little is known about the origins of Egyptian religion. It is known that from the time when Egypt was united under a single ruler—Menes (also called Narmer), around 2850 B.C.—the society was ruled by a god, the pharaoh. He did not rule by divine right, he was divine; he was almighty; he was omnipotent. And he embodied Egypt. The pharaoh assumed for himself the responsibility of governing and protecting the country, but his price was high; the primary purpose of the lives he governed and protected was his own aggrandizement. Every enterprise of Egyptian life was controlled by him and was given to him.

The Egyptians' attitude toward pharaoh—and pharaoh's attitude about himself—not only influenced the architecture that grew up in Egypt; it shaped it. For Egyptian architecture is so monumental that it is really more monument than it is architecture.

All architecture is monumental: the Hanging Gardens were a monument to Babylon; the Cathedral of Chartres is a monument to the Virgin Mary, the Roman Catholic church, and the pious town of Chartres; the Chase Manhattan Bank Building is a monument to the Chase Manhattan Bank. But these three examples also serve, or served, some real architectural purpose. Scholars may argue about which function is the more important, but at least they can agree that both exist.

Standing guard in the midst of the desert, the Great Sphinx (above) seems to act like a watchdog for the pyramids in the background. Even though the pyramids have been mapped and charted (above, right), they still retain a special kind of eternal mystery, as was caught in the nineteenth-century drawing (right) of early explorers delving into a pyramid seeking its burial chamber.

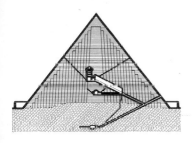

As for the Egyptian pyramids, however, one might argue that those behemoths of antiquity were not even architecture, but rather monumental sculpture. For many of the pyramids did not enclose space at all: the pyramid of King Zoser, for instance, is a completely solid structure built over a mastaba—the early form of the Egyptian tomb.

Be that as it may, the great pyramids of Egypt were colossal structures; and they certainly minced no words describing who was in charge there. Constructed of sandstone rock so perfectly cut that no mortar was necessary, the largest of the monuments covered approximately twelve acres and rose nearly five hundred feet from its base. As many as one hundred thousand laborers were employed—or impressed into the pharaoh's service—for the projects, which took approximately twenty years.

The pyramids contained burial chambers for the mummified body of the pharaoh, and perhaps his wife, and storerooms for the luxuries the dead would require in the sublime afterlife. But these monuments did not stand in isolation on the Egyptian desert, as they do today; they were parts of enormous funerary districts with temples and courtyards where religious observances were held even during the pharaohs' lifetimes. Virtually all of the Egyptians' architectural efforts were concentrated on these complexes; until quite late in the history of ancient Egypt the capital cities and even the palaces of the pharaohs were comparatively humble.

By far the greatest of the funerary districts—and one of the artistic and engineering marvels of the world—was at Giza. There, in the twenty-sixth century B.C., the pyramids of Mycerinus, Chephren, and Cheops were built side-by-side, and about a third of mile away another wonder was included as part of the complex: the Great Sphinx. Seen today, the Giza structures are impressive enough. But imagine them back when they were just completed, towering over a series of temples and courts and causeways, everything except the guardian Sphinx—which was carved from a spur of rock—gleaming white against the vast sepia landscape. Originally the three Giza pyramids and their attendant structures were faced with limestone; according to observers the stone was so highly polished and the seams so perfectly matched that each side presented a smooth, unbroken surface. Unfortunately, the facing was removed a slab at a time (although some remains at the top of Mycerinus's pyramid) by the builders of Cairo—which was a travesty, especially inasmuch as the cliffs nearby were still rich in limestone.

For centuries the great pyramids of Egypt have been objects of intriguing mystery. Some of the mysteries contained within the pyramids have been pirated, and as a result museums throughout Europe and the United States have made the contents of the ancient tombs familiar and a good deal less mysterious. Nevertheless, the ancient structures retain as many secrets as they have given up. No one has yet figured out the significance of their placement. The base of a pyramid is a square, and (with the exception of one minor pyramid) each square is placed so that each side faces one of the cardinal points. Did, then, the pyramids serve some function not generally recognized, perhaps related to astronomy or engineering? No one knows for sure. The slope of each

The likenesses of three great pharaohs, from left to right Mycerinus, Cheops, and Chephren, stare out through the ages, as do their timeless monuments, viewed below in the same order.

pyramid is subtly varied. Mycerinus's pyramid rises at an angle of 51°; Chephren's slope is 52° 20′, and Cheops's is 51° 52′. The reason for the difference is unknown, but few scholars who know the ancient Egyptians would suggest that it was arbitrary.

Another mystery is the actual shape of the pyramids. Each side of a pyramid is not precisely the flat, equilateral triangle it appears to be. Actually, each side is a pair of right triangles, almost, but not quite precisely, back-to-back: their bases extend slightly outward from the juncture of the two right angles. Is this arrangement related to the placement of the pyramid? It could be, for, given the placement of the pyramid base, each juncture of right angles corresponds to a main compass point. But the reason remains elusive.

Apparently the pyramids at Giza were sufficiently intimidating to dissuade subsequent pharaohs from trying to equal or surpass their colossal presence. Several more pyramids were built, but the scale grew

steadily smaller, and many of the rulers looked for different kinds of places in which to enjoy their afterlives. Some chose to follow the example of the submonarchial nobility and build cubic, rock-hewn tombs; others decided to take advantage of the rock mountains west of the Nile valley and have their tombs dug deep within the natural formations. These were not simply man-made caves, but cavernous chambers, elaborately appointed, and guarded by funerary districts and temple complexes that were more conventionally architectural.

One of the grandest of these cliffside complexes was the mortuary temple of Queen Hatshepsut, built near Thebes in the sixteenth century B.C. Even as a ruin, the structure reveals its monumentality and complexity; one can still make out the long processional avenue, guarded by sphinxes, that led gently upward from the valley to the base of the cliff. The ramps are still there, leading up to each of the three massive terraces, which are fronted with double colonnades, rows of the falsely

Among the more spectacular Egyptian ruins is the tomb of Queen Hatshepsut (below) dating from the sixteenth century B.C. and built at Deir el-Bahri on the Nile. Much of the force of the structure is derived from the manner in which its builders utilized the grandeur of the site. On the other bank of the Nile, at Luxor, stands a temple (right) to the important god Amen-re, who also had a vast temple complex at Karnak.

cylindrical, usually sixteen-sided columns that would, much later, evolve into the Greek column known as Doric. Sanctuaries with gigantic altars to the gods are accessible from the terraces; walls are carved with friezes that depict Hatshepsut's divine birth and her achievements as a ruler; portals and capitals are embellished with leaf motifs—another foretaste of Classical Greece. From the uppermost terrace a corridor cuts into the rock cliff and leads to the chief sanctuary deep within.

Perhaps for reasons of camouflage—grave robbing may already have been a profitable vocation—the actual tomb is quite a distance away from the temple complex, but it is linked by a relatively inconspicuous avenue that becomes another corridor into the rock. At the end of the corridor is a rough, cavelike room, and behind the cavelike room is the entrance to the vault where Hatshepsut's mummy was placed, surrounded by all the luxuries she would need in her afterlife. The vault is blue, and although today there is nothing in it, its emptiness is eloquent. For if no evidence remains of the mummified queen and her belongings, neither is there any sign of the modern world within the chamber—no jet-age sights or sounds. Maybe it is the very isolation of the chamber and the silence within, or maybe the familiar Egyptian scarab blue is responsible, but inside the vault there is an aura inexplicably Egyptian. The blue emptiness and the silence encourage thoughts to drift off, back, and to sense just a little of the timeless quality one associates with ancient Egypt, a world where life went on but never seemed to change.

3

Civicism and Classicism

THAT THE ARCHITECTURE of ancient Greece was influenced by the architecture of ancient Mesopotamia and Egypt is not news. It has been apparent all along to anyone in a position to compare the buildings of the Near and Middle East. What is news, relatively speaking, is how the influence was transported.

Until the present century, scholars believed that the various architectural motifs, techniques, and conventions that originated in Mesopotamia and Egypt and later appeared in Greece were transported by the peoples—Dorians, Ionians, Aeolians, Achaeans, among others—who traversed the eastern Mediterranean area in the second millennium B.C. before settling in Thrace and the Peloponnesus. This assumption held up for centuries; if the first Greek immigrants did not import the architecture from the East, who else could have? Nowadays we know better than did earlier historians how the influence moved west: it was carried westward in the sailing ships of the Minoans, one of the most extraordinary people of the ancient world.

Before 1900, very little was known about the Minoans—only that they had lived on the island of Crete, that their civilization had flourished after about 2000 B.C. and had disappeared rather mysteriously around 1400 B.C. It was generally assumed that they were related to the Mycenaean Greeks who lived on the mainland at the same time. Then, at the start of our own century a British archaeologist, Arthur Evans, began excavating on Crete. In one of the most sensational and successful excavations in history, Evans uncovered—and then supervised the restoration of—the vast labyrinth complex at Knossos, consisting of the Palace of King Minos, a marketplace, and a town. And when the restoration was completed, the Minoans were no longer strangers. Such is the documentary power of architecture; almost everything we know about the Minoans we have learned from the architecture of Knossos—and we know quite a bit.

(In the interest of accuracy it should perhaps be noted that some of the most revealing evidence found at Knossos is not, technically, architectural. For example, on some stone slabs that were dug up was one kind of writing, similar to the writing of the Mycenaeans, and on other slabs was writing completely unrelated to early Greek. Scholars have speculated that therefore the Minoans may not have been an Aegean race at all and probably learned the proto-Greek writing in order to

The origins of the Palace of King Minos at Knossos are shrouded by time, but we do know that it was rebuilt around 1600 B.C. At that time extensive servants' quarters were added, suggesting a new degree of affluence had come to Minoan society. The apogee of that culture was in the following two centuries. The view at left shows the northern entrance of the palace as it looks today.

deal with their Mycenaean neighbors. Similarly, the restored murals at Knossos describe a great deal about the daily life of the Minoans—their agricultural and maritime vocations and their fascination with sport, especially bull jumping. Of course, the murals are part of the walls, but whether or not they should be counted as architectural is moot.)

Knossos is a modular complex, set on the side of a hill, facing the sea. No walls surround the town, so the Minoans must not have been troubled by invaders. (Some murals depict soldiers, however, hence there was a military establishment of some sort and, of course, there was a navy.) At the center of the palace section is a large open court surrounded by royal apartments, a throne room, and various state rooms, most colonnaded in a style not dissimilar to that used in the Egyptian temple complexes. The bastion and guard house, incidentally, are tiny, possibly indicating a low rate of political crime. A west wing contains a series of storerooms stocked with huge earthenware jars that probably held exotic oils, domestic and imported, in which the Minoans may have traded. Thousands of inscribed clay tablets were found in the archives situated at the northern end of the complex. Behind the archives is the theatrical area, a series of large and small arenas used for sporting events, plays, and concerts. The market on the west side is large and paved. But one of the most remarkable features of Knossos is the plumbing system; the apartments contained bathrooms with running water and flush toilets—perhaps the first in the world.

If the impression given by the architecture is correct, the Minoans were a secure and prosperous people, conscientious in their business enterprises, but with plenty of leisure time, which they put to good use. They liked sports, music, dancing, and although they probably were fairly religious, their religion apparently demanded little self-denial and did not frown on such earthly pleasures as gambling and drinking. Their murals and figure carvings reveal a lusty appreciation of the human body and an occasional attraction to bizarre—and seductive—costumes. Finally, the very openness of the labyrinth structure suggests that the rulers were more accessible to the people than was the case in most societies of the time; aristocrat, farmer, sailor, and trader may well have mingled in the marketplace, theater, and arena, sharing many of the same goods and pleasures.

The glories of Greek building extend from the Mycenaean Lion Gate (below) to the peerless Parthenon (opposite), whose frieze included such monumental bas-reliefs as the horsemen (above left).

Overleaf: Access to the Acropolis is by the Panathenaic Way, which rises some three-hundred yards to the top, where it enters the Propylaea, a combined gate and temple.

A democratic society? Certainly not. Nevertheless, Knossos is a long way, in miles and spirit, from the Egyptian complexes—however similar their colonnades. For Knossos is a civic center, constructed and maintained for use by the entire population. And so, before they mysteriously disappeared, the Minoans gave two things to the mainland Greeks: the architectural traditions they had picked up from the Mesopotamians and Egyptians; and an idea that would become a Greek and then, more conspicuously, a Roman tradition—that monumental architecture could also be civic architecture.

Anyone with even a cursory acquaintanceship with the best-known monuments of ancient Greece may find himself questioning the designation of Greek architecture as "civic." After all, most of the structures are temples: no secular architecture of any real significance appears until the Hellenistic age. One justifies the designation in two ways. First, the Greek temples were not isolated, but generally belonged to a complex of buildings constructed around a vast, paved plaza that often functioned as an urban gathering place. A city like Athens would house two such complexes: at the acropolis, or highest point, would be a temenos, a sacred, walled enclosure where the most important local temples would stand and which would also serve as a citadel from which approaching invaders could be spotted; and in the lower city there would be an agora, or marketplace, also defined by temples. The actual function of each of the major buildings may not have related to civic purposes, but the clustering of the temples had the effect of defining the location where civic matters were conducted. When the Romans adopted the Greek approach to urban construction, they formalized and emphasized the function of the plazas, at least when they had the opportunity to start from scratch. They defined the open space first, and then laid out the buildings around it. One of the results of this was the Roman forum.

But there is a second way in which to justify the civic designation of Greek architecture, and it probably is the more significant. To understand it, however, we have to remember with whom we are dealing. The Greeks were not the down-to-earth Minoans, nor were they the more literal, more practical Romans. They were a people who produced Plato and Aristotle, Sophocles and Euripides, Empedocles and Hippocrates; they were, in other words, the great intellectuals of antiquity, as concerned with the essence as with the application of ideas. And so to the Greeks, who liked definitions and formulas for the achievement of ideals, the notion of civic architecture could not have meant anything as simple as architecture with a public function. Civic architecture had to be architecture that in essence created a relationship between itself and the civic body—people. The primary means employed to achieve this ideal was scale. Greek architecture, in sum, was civic architecture primarily because it had a civic, or human, scale.

The basic form of Greek architecture was the megaron, a structure with a rectangular plan, a porch along the façade or at least before the entrance, and a pitched gable roof. Although not absolutely unique to the Greek mainland, the megaron was built there in earliest times—the form has been found in the oldest strata of Troy, which dates from

The Erechtheum (above), built in the Ionic order, is noted for its Caryatid Porch, graced by six draped female figures. (Today only five are authentic; the sixth is a replacement for one that was abducted and confined in the British Museum.) The orders of Greek architecture, shown at left, are (from the top) Doric, Ionic, and Corinthian.

2700 B.C.—and was well suited to the climatic conditions and available materials (mainly timber) of the region. During the Mycenaean age the megaron was probably quite ubiquitous as the central form in the primitive, fortified castles built by the warrior-princes whose conflicts are described in the *Iliad* and *Odyssey*. After the Trojan War, which ended around 1100 B.C., Mycenae was destroyed. A dark age enveloped mainland Greece, and like Europe's later Dark Ages it was characterized by barbarian invasions and a virtually total cessation of building. Three centuries of cultural interaction followed, and when the darkness lifted and the Greeks began to build again, the megaron reappeared. Now, however, there were other architectural elements that the Greeks wished to employ in their structures—the Egyptian colonnade, for example, which remained on the Mycenaean ruins; for the Mycenaeans had learned it from the Minoans, who had imported the idea from the Middle East.

In any case, between the eighth and sixth centuries B.C., the basic elements of Greek architecture steadily blended. The megaron widened; stone replaced wood; the roof was extended, sometimes all around the megaron in order to create a deeper porch, and therefore the colonnade surrounded the entire structure. Certain stylistic differences developed as the building of temples became a national pastime in Greece. Some architects preferred a style in which great emphasis was placed on the perfect balance between horizontal and vertical members. Character-

Athena Nike, the Greek goddess of victory, was portrayed as wingless (below) to prevent her from flying away in time of need. Her temple (left) on the Acropolis in Athens well illustrates the Ionic style, as against the simpler Doric of the Temple at Segesta, Sicily (opposite).

ized by straight lines and sharp, angular contrasts, this style was known as Doric, since it was believed to have been formulated by the Dorian people who had settled the Peloponnesus. Another style was the Ionic, named for the Ionians who lived on the coasts of Asia Minor. Much less massive than the Doric, the graceful Ionic is more richly decorated and owes much more to the Egyptians. Moreover, sharp contrasts were avoided or concealed in the Ionic. Whereas a Doric column is placed on a simple circular base and has a simple rectangular capital—features that stress right angles—an Ionic column sits on a gently molded base and has a scroll-type or foliate capital to soften the angularity of the junctures. Later, in the fifth century B.C., certain elements of Doric and Ionic architecture were merged and the Corinthian style evolved. It is thought to have been named for a metalworker from Corinth who invented the distinctive carved-leaf capital motif, and is the lightest and most decorative of the three architectural forms.

The Greeks did not call the three styles "styles;" they called them orders. And orders are just what they were; formalized, carefully defined, constantly refined systems designed to achieve a prescribed end —specifically, architecture scaled so that a human being could relate to it. Rooms could never be so small as to seem confining, nor so large as to allow the occupant to lose himself in their spaciousness. If the function of a room dictated spaciousness—an inordinately high ceiling, for instance—then measures were taken to reduce the illusion of vastness. The room might be banded with horizontal molding at a specific height to make the walls seem less high. No façade was either so wide or so high that it could not be perceived at once in its entirety.

Even the placement of buildings was calculated to create an intimacy between architecture and people. Generally a building was sited in relation to its main approach so that the oncoming visitor could see two sides and thus instantly comprehend the building's whole scale. Greek architects even employed a certain deception in order to strengthen the illusion of regularity. Because columns tend to look narrower against a light, bright background than against a dark, shadowed background, Greek builders often made the columns at the extremes of the colonnaded portico thicker than those at the center (the outermost columns were generally seen against a background of sky, while the others were backed by the building itself). The formalization of the orders and the consequent evolution of a standardized, civic scale produced what the Greeks regarded as an ideal architecture—and what we continue to call Classical architecture. And their opinion of their own achievement has been endorsed by many subsequent societies, who have created any number of Neoclassical periods down through history. Indeed, Classical architecture is probably the closest thing there is to an official secular architecture of Western civilization.

The necessary use of the word "secular" in that last sentence is revealing (as revealing for what it says about Western civilization as about Greek architecture). Almost all of the Greeks' greatest buildings were temples: the three great monuments on the Acropolis in Athens (the Temple of Athena Nike, the Erechtheum, and the peerless Parthenon); the Olympeum in lower Athens; the temples of Concord and

Segesta in Sicily; Poseidon's shrine in southern Italy and Apollo's in Asia Minor. These were religious edifices, and yet when a religion capable of sweeping through Western civilization came along, became institutionalized, and began building monuments to itself, it turned away from Classical architecture and came up with something else. Several historical and logistical matters contributed to this rejection, but the most important reason why Classical architecture was not suited to the needs of institutionalized Christianity may have been its civic scale.

The Greeks, after all, had a tendency to idealize things, while simultaneously reducing them to a human scale. (Even the Greek gods and goddesses, as represented in mythology and art, were eminently human —human sized, motivated by human needs and ambitions, superhuman in their vices and virtues. Temples built to a human scale were perfectly well suited to such deities.) This tendency was reflected in the development of Greek building, and the result was Classical architecture, an architecture almost wholly devoid of intrinsic emotional potency. When a building is perfectly proportioned, when none of its parts is too large or too small, when its horizontal, vertical, and diagonal members strike an equal balance, when optical illusions are employed for the purpose of ensuring the appearance of regularity, then that building has no facility of its own to induce feelings. Intellectual admiration, yes, but no subjective feelings; Classical architecture does not awe, it does not overwhelm, it does not entertain. As an emotional catalyst it is—it is meant to be—neutral. Whatever subjective feelings were later stimulated by the Classical idiom were stimulated by associations, not by architecture. When the builders of Washington, D.C., decided to use the Classical style for the federal buildings, they were eager to impart a Greco-Roman grandeur to the capital of the young nation; but the grandeur was that of Greece and Rome, not of the architecture.

Classical architecture, then, was not what the Christians had in mind when they started building monumental edifices. For the Christian hierarchy—first in the Byzantine East and then in the late medieval West —wanted religious architecture to do something to the emotions of people; to intimidate and inspire, threaten and reassure, awe and comfort, all at once. Faced with these goals, Classical architecture did not stand a chance. Its civic associations lingered, though, and it did become the dominant style of Christendom's secular buildings.

Actually, the Romans were probably more responsible than the Greeks for establishing the civic associations of the Classical idiom. It is true that the Greeks invented Classical architecture and gave it its civic scale, but in the hands of the Romans it became more conspicuously civic in function. Moreover, the Romans turned the Classical into the world's first international style; long after the fall of Rome, Roman Classical architecture remained in lands that had once belonged to the empire. From Britain, France, and Germany to Egypt and Syria, in Spain, across North Africa, and into Asia Minor the Roman buildings stood, familiar to populations and influential to generation after generation of architects.

The Romans have not had a good press. According to the conven-

In order to supply their vast public baths, as well as fill household needs, the Romans needed water in large amounts for their cities. Drawing on their considerable skill as engineers, they constructed aqueducts so sturdy and well-built that many, including the one at Segovia, Spain (above), built about A.D. 10, stand to this day.

tional historical wisdom, the Greeks were the truly sensitive ones, the more intellectual and artistically gifted people who devised the formulas that produced Classical art. The Romans were mere imitators. Impressed with the excellence of Greek art, they imported Greek artists and had their own artists copy Greek models in the hope that the achievements of the Greeks would be seen as theirs. Worse, the Romans adopted the Classical idiom not because they had any genuine appreciation of Classical aesthetics, but for propaganda purposes. The Classical monuments they erected throughout their empire were primarily proclamations of their dominance, advertisements for themselves.

The conventional wisdom is not exactly wrong, but it is, to say the least, harsh. In fact, the Roman approach to architecture was approximately the same as the Roman approach to everything else: always practical, somewhat pompous, generally realistic. At the time of their emergence as the mightiest power on earth, they had no native artistic traditions to speak of. They had aspirations, however, and wished to match their political and military superiority with a display of cultural wealth. Greece had the traditions, so Rome simply adopted them as its own. Thenceforth the Romans would call themselves the inheritors of Greek culture, just as, when Rome itself would later fall, the barbarian invaders would call themselves the inheritors of Roman culture.

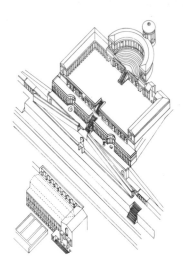

But the Romans did more than simply pick up the Greeks' artistic traditions and spread them around; they contributed to the further development of the building art, especially its engineering aspects. The Greeks had used a basic post-and-lintel system of construction almost exclusively; to this the Romans added a perfected system of arch and vault construction. As a result a much greater variety of buildings appeared, each with a form suited to its function. Unlike the Greeks, the Romans undertook enormous public works projects, including a vast network of bridges and much-needed aqueducts. Perhaps more significantly, the Romans began building on a truly urban scale; they were cognizant of the relationships between buildings, and of the effect of buildings on open space. Indeed, when Roman builders had the opportunity to start from scratch—as when they erected towns in the colonies —they clearly viewed forums and other outdoor spaces as architectural elements every bit as important as temple walls and domes.

For all intents and purposes, Roman architecture was a product of the empire. During the era of the republic, which was established in 509 B.C., most of Rome's energy was devoted to military enterprises. Whatever building needed to be done was generally executed in the utilitarian Etruscan tradition, probably by Etruscan builders. Although

little remains, the republican building was undoubtedly brick, and is important because of the development of the arch, the continuous arch, and the arched vault that had been used by the Etruscans for centuries.

After their conquest of Greece, completed in 146 B.C., the Romans began to move in the direction of the Greek models in their building projects. Within fifty years they had developed a distinctive kind of architecture that contained the basic elements that would characterize the building of imperial Rome; the spirit and sculptural qualities of Greek Classical architecture combined with the traditions of Romanized Etruscan architecture and expressed in the colossal scale that the Romans so dearly loved. One of the first expressions of the emerging Roman style was the Sanctuary of Fortuna Primigenia, erected in the Apennine foothills of Palestrina, east of Rome, in the first century B.C.

This gigantic complex of ramps, terraces, colonnades, and vaults—comparable in scale and setting to the temple complex of Queen Hatshepsut in Egypt—is notable not only for its monumentality but for what it reveals about the Romans' splendid sense of the relationships between architectural forms, open space, and site. The Palestrina complex seems to have been slipped over an entire hillside the way a glove slips over a hand. The open spaces between structures appear to duplicate the open spaces between formations in the craggy surrounding landscape; the structures themselves have a direct, even subservient relationship to the shape of the land—the uppermost, central structure, a gabled temple (see reconstruction at left), was built so that its peak would be just slightly lower in altitude than the top of the hill. Antici-

The Sanctuary of Fortuna Primigenia at Palestrina had been abandoned and forgotten and a whole new village had been built over it. Then, in an Allied bombing raid of World War II, the new was blasted away and the old uncovered. It has since been excavated (below) and experts have reconstructed the way it looked (left).

Overleaf: *A modern model of ancient, imperial Rome shows the Circus Maximus (center) and the Colosseum (upper right).*

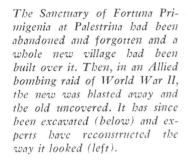

pating the often-quoted dictum of Frank Lloyd Wright, the builders at Palestrina obviously believed that "architecture is an extension of the environment."

At the risk of belaboring the point, one might find it instructive, when comparing the essential differences between Greek and Roman builders, to contrast the Palestrina sanctuary with the greatest of the Greek architectural complexes, the Acropolis at Athens. Both complexes consist of several temples and secondary structures situated on a hill and united by paved surfaces. But the difference in the way the parts of each are joined to make a structural whole, and the difference in the way the aesthetic integrity of each is achieved reveal the entirely different conceptual basis from which the builders operated. At the Acropolis each building is an independent entity, a work of art in itself; the Erechtheum would be just as beautiful (though not nearly as impressive) if it were standing someplace else. The physical unity of the Acropolis is achieved by the wall that surrounds it, by the walkways connecting the buildings, and by the hilltop site itself. Its aesthetic unity is the product of the stylistic elements that establish a kinship between the buildings, of the composition of the parts, and the harmony of all the proportions.

At Palestrina, on the other hand, it is difficult to tell where one part ends and another begins. The sanctuary is a physical whole, conceived and constructed as a single unit, with space volumes and connections between enclosures designed as architectural elements. Thus the two complexes clearly reveal not only the very different architectural approaches of their creators, but also the very different character and attitudes of the two peoples. The Greeks, it might be said, built the Acropolis the way one might build a sculpture garden; they made sure that everything was compatible, but their primary concern was that each work of art should be displayed to its best advantage and for its own sake. The Romans built a monument—a single, strong, unified entity, a whole of parts, indivisible—not unlike the empire itself.

Of course, when the Sanctuary of Fortuna Primigenia was built, the Roman Empire had not yet been declared. It did exist, though, for Rome had already conquered most of the territory over which it would rule for four hundred years. In fact, the sanctuary at Palestrina was probably built by Sulla, the consul whose dictatorship (83–79 B.C.) is regarded as transitional in the process that converted Rome from a republic to an empire with strong one-man rule. In any case, Roman nationalism certainly existed by the time the sanctuary was built, and it colored every aspect of Roman activity, architecture included.

Unfortunately, once the empire was declared, the Palestrina monument gradually fell into disuse. The rulers of imperial Rome tended to concentrate their building activity either in Rome itself, which they were determined to make the grandest city in world history, or in colonial outposts, to improve the efficiency and comfort of Roman procurators and, just as importantly, to remind colonial populations of who was in charge there. Palestrina was not quite close enough to home to warrant the maintenance it required, but neither was it far enough away, so gradually it started to crumble. Parts of it fell away, and the rest of it became buried under layers of dust and clay. In medieval times some Italians decided that the site was suitable for a village, and before long the village had grown into a fair-sized town. Then in 1944, a squadron of Allied bombers flew over what was still a fair-sized town and within minutes most of Palestrina was blasted off the face of the earth. However, some of the earth had been blasted away in the unfortunate bombing of the town, and there lay the substantial remains of the Sanctuary of Fortuna Primigenia.

The Roman Empire was declared in 27 B.C., and the first official Roman emperor, Augustus Caesar, immediately launched a construction program to make Rome a worthy capital. Augustus liked to say that he found Rome a city of brick and would leave it a city of marble, and it was not an idle boast. All over the city mud-brick and stucco buildings were replaced by superbly built stone monuments. If it was true that Rome was not built in a day—or even in a single regency (Augustus ruled until A.D. 14)—it was also true that its new, grand

Over the many long centuries of its existence, Rome has undergone great transformations. Above left: the A.D. 82 Arch of Titus, as painted in 1871 by George Healy showing at left the poet Henry Wadsworth Longfellow with his daughter "Edith with golden hair." Two views of the Forum Romanum include a painting from the sixteenth century (left) and a modern photograph (above).

imperial character was achieved very quickly. Moreover, the urban renewal programs undertaken by Augustus became a continuous process as subsequent Caesars determined to make the city even more magnificent—and, not incidentally, to leave their own individual marks for later generations.

Rome had always been built around a forum, an open marketplace, into which main thoroughfares converged and around which buildings were grouped. By the time of Julius Caesar, the old forum (the Forum Romanum) was so overcrowded and so inadequate as a public and commercial gathering place that in 54 B.C. he built a new, larger forum. Unlike the Forum Romanum, which had more or less evolved on its own, the Forum of Julius Caesar was carefully planned. It consisted of a large plaza enclosed on four sides by a portico housing shops. When Augustus became Caesar, he also built a forum in his own honor. He placed a large temple at one end and a statue of himself in the open square. Not every subsequent emperor had a forum built for himself. but enough did to make imperial Rome, for all its notorious congestion, a remarkably airy city.

Although most of the imperial forums contained a temple, religious buildings were not terribly important to Rome. In their own way the Romans were religious, but theirs were rather undefined religions, based more on superstition than theology. The Romans continued to build magnificent temples; grandiloquence was characteristic of the

51

Romans—they would not build anything simply that they could build on a grand scale. But in the overall scheme of things, the basilicas were more important.

The Roman basilica was the principal civic building; it contained commercial exchanges, the halls of justice, and, on occasion, quarters for the bureaucracy. Generally square or rectilinear in plan, it contained a large, open central area called a nave, which was flanked by pillars and roofed with an arched vault or dome. On the exterior side of the pillars, which supported the round arches, were long aisles, which sometimes were partitioned off to form individual rooms opening onto the nave. A great deal of variation marked the construction of the basilicas; at the gigantic Basilica of Trajan in Rome, the extremities were finished with rounded sections called apses. Not until much later, in medieval times, did the basilican plan characterized by the rectangular shape, vaulted nave, and apse become standardized; to the Romans, "basilica" was more likely to define function than form.

Acknowledging some of the traits that typified most of their subjects, the Roman emperors made certain that their building programs provided an adequate number of theaters, amphitheaters, and circuses for Rome. For the Romans were great spectators. The enjoyed drama, loved sports, and were enraptured by animal acts. They also had a penchant for pageantry and a notorious streak of brutality, both of which were satisfied by the enormous displays staged in the arenas: the death-dealing combat of the gladiators; the fast, deafening, unpredictable chariot races; and, when the time came, the one-sided, quite predictable confrontations between hungry lions and Christian martyrs. Such spectacles, quite naturally, had to be conducted in appropriately spectacular enclosures.

For a while the Theater of Marcellus, completed in 11 B.C., was suitable. Semicircular, it rose in three tiers around a half-circle stage. Interestingly, on the exterior of the theater the Romans used a different Greek order for each row of columns. On the ground story Doric columns stand between the continuous arches; on the middle level the

Ionic was employed; and at the top (which has not survived), Corinthian. Exactly why the Romans chose to use all three orders together is not really clear. It has been suggested that they wanted to demonstrate their awareness of the sequential development of the Classical forms imported from Greece, and also to broadcast their own aesthetic sensibility, which was sound enough to successfully blend the three orders into a unified whole. Whatever the reason, the combining of the three orders became something of a convention in Roman theater and amphitheater building. It was expressed most dramatically at the Colosseum, the massive oval begun in A.D. 70 because the Theater of Marcellus was proving wholly inadequate to accommodate the fast-growing scale of the local entertainments.

The ruin that remains today gives some suggestion of the size and structural properties of the Colosseum, but in its heyday it was best known for its decorative richness. In addition to the superimposed orders that divide the round arches, the huge structure was embellished with marble sheathing and shiny bronze medallions; and in the arches of the upper stories were marble statues of Roman soldiers. Approaches, portals, arcades, corridors, and stairways to the interior tiers were so carefully thought out that a full house—about sixty thousand Romans—could vacate the premises in a matter of minutes. Cells for wild beasts and gladiators were constructed beneath the arena, which, incidentally, could be flooded for crocodile hunts and naval displays. Large as it was, the Colosseum was not really well suited to chariot races and horse races, and so the Circus Maximus was built. This structure was 2,000 feet long and 650 feet wide, with straight sides and rounded ends and a seating capacity of 125,000 people. By the fourth century a series of enlargements had increased the capacity to 385,000! Sad to say, nothing of the Circus Maximus remains but the open space it enclosed.

In all, the Romans are known to have built at least seventy amphitheaters throughout the empire, and a number of small theaters for drama. The only other kind of building that may have come close to that quantity was the thermae, or baths. If Roman citizens had had a bill of rights, the right to an elaborate bath might have been article one; for a thermae was built in every consequential outpost in the empire, even in the northern colonies where frequent bathing was less essential than it was in the hot and humid Mediterranean lands.

None of the thermae was a simple structure; the complicated plumbing and the systems employed to control air temperatures precluded structural simplicity, as did the bathing procedure itself. Each thermae contained dressing rooms; a *palaestra*, a sort of gymnasium used for physical exercise before bathing; a pair of steambaths; a series of small rooms for scrubbing, oiling, and massage; and three principal rooms, much larger than the others, the *frigidarium*, *tepidarium*, and *calidarium*. The *frigidarium*, not surprisingly, was an unheated pool; the *tepidarium* was a vaulted lounge containing tepid running-water baths; and the *calidarium* was a circular, domed enclosure in which the air, as well as the water in the pool, was kept quite hot. The larger and later thermae—epitomized by the Baths of Caracalla, built in Rome

The baths built on the order of the emperor Caracalla, completed in A.D. 217, accommodated sixteen hundred bathers at a time. The reconstruction (right) gives some idea of its monumentality. Now largely ruins (below), it has been used in modern times as an amphitheater in which to stage operas.

early in the third century—also contained garden courtyards, conference rooms, game rooms, small art galleries, and libraries; and they were the official headquarters for one of the grandest of the Romans' many pageants, the Bacchanalian orgy.

It is a pity that so little remains of the many thermae that the Romans built throughout their world; for of all Roman architecture, the baths in some important ways were the most characteristically Roman. The Baths of Caracalla, for example, is as expressive of the Romans' sense of design unity as the sanctuary at Palestrina or any of the imperial forums. It demonstrates the Romans' ability to mold solid and space volumes into a whole of separate and yet inseparable parts. This quality can be discerned from surviving copies of plans and from archaeological reconstructions. Moreover, documents and a few extant fragments of floors, walls, and statuary suggest something of the lavishness of the interiors. But how sumptuous the whole thermae must have been—that we can only imagine, although the chances are that our imaginations would fall short. The thermae was the one place where the Romans' tastes could be fully satisfied.

A temple had to be restrained, dignified. A basilica had to reflect the majestic sobriety and strength of the government. An amphitheater or circus could be decorated a little more loosely, but the functional demands of those places really dictated and dominated the form. At the thermae, decoration was part of the form; at the thermae the Romans' love of ostentatious luxury was given free reign. There were marble colonnades and abundant statuary; walls were stuccoed and painted with bright-colored murals depicting the various secular pleasures of Roman life; floors were paved with glazed mosaic inlaid with marble; deeply molded coffers decorated the vaulted ceilings; geometric or floriate patterns were incised or molded or painted wherever there was wall space otherwise unaccounted for. The pure display of opulence was purely Roman. Indeed, the thermae, like the decoration that embellished it, like the elaborate baths taken and the orgies held within it, expressed much more clearly than any other element of Roman architecture a seemingly fundamental precept of Roman life: excess is not nearly enough.

4

New Rome...and New Romans

THERE IS NOTHING EXCESSIVE about the Pantheon. Large and imposing as it is, it is above all else a masterpiece of restraint, a perfectly proportioned edifice without an ounce of fat. Some things about it seem to synthesize Roman architecture; the superb engineering, for instance, and the massing of contrasting shapes in a unified whole. But something else about it suggests that the Pantheon is almost the antithesis of everything conventionally associated with Roman architecture. Perhaps it is its spirit that makes it different (different, certainly, from the thermae). The Pantheon is grand, but grand in a solemn, temperate way; it is bold, without being arrogant; it is noble in an understated way that bears no pomposity. Indeed, the exterior of the Pantheon is scarcely ornamented at all; from most angles it appears a simple, solid, cylindrical drum of reinforced concrete capped with a dome. From the front one sees a handsome but unextraordinary portico with eight Corinthian columns supporting a low entablature and a fairly steep pediment, trimmed but otherwise undecorated. And so you have a building that is attractive, clean, beautifully proportioned—but a masterpiece? Not until you see it on the inside.

Even inside, the source of the Pantheon's splendor is hard to identify. Is it the surprising depth of the dome, which turns out to be a complete hemisphere set on the second tier of the three-tiered cylindrical substructure? Or is it the ethereal lighting, which animates the coffers of the dome (these are not merely decorative, they substantially reduce the weight of the concrete dome) and glistens on the gilt surfaces of the rotunda? This is a possibility, especially as there are no windows in the Pantheon and only one source of light—an opening, or oculus, in the top of the dome. Or perhaps the source of this elusive yet undeniably real splendor comes from something else, something intangible—space itself.

However elusive, the special quality that makes the Pantheon the masterpiece it is exists. It was recognized, and it was emulated. Unfortunately, we do not know who was responsible for creating it. The Pantheon, a temple dedicated to "all the gods," or, specifically, to the seven planetary gods, was originally built in 25 B.C. by Agrippa, the son-in-law of Augustus Caesar, but was almost totally destroyed by fire late in the first century A.D. Hadrian undertook reconstruction in A.D. 120, and another addition and restoration were inaugurated by Septimius

The Roman penchant for excess is noticeably absent in the graceful proportions of the Pantheon, the supreme monument of Roman architecture. The stark simplicity of the fluted Corinthian columns (left) that adorn the edifice's interior are tribute indeed to the genius of its anonymous architect.

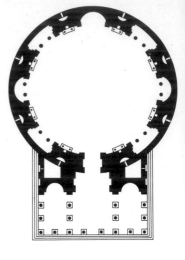

Severus in 202. Most scholars speculate that the portico dates from the original temple, the rotunda from the time of Hadrian, and the dome in its present form from the third century—which, if true, makes the unified design of the Pantheon especially remarkable. In any case, the building obviously meant a great deal to the Romans, for it has remained one of the best cared for of all ancient structures. (In the seventh century, Pope Boniface IV had the pagan statuary and much of the ornamentation removed from the interior and converted the edifice into a Christian church. Today the Pantheon, still in excellent condition, is known officially as the Church of Santa Maria Rotonda.)

If you had lived in Rome in the third century, you might well have recognized the extraordinary beauty of the Pantheon, but you would not have realized how important the building would be to the continuing development of architecture. For that you would have needed centuries of historical information, for the Pantheon's influence was subtle, took a good while to catch hold, and was not necessarily apparent in Rome itself.

Then again, if you had lived in Rome in the third century, you might well have been thinking of other things. Politically and economically the government was coming apart. The relative peace that had prevailed in most of the empire since the imperial era began was breaking down. In the West, there were rebellions in Britain, and an endless trickle of troublesome Germanic nomads kept eroding the strength of the Roman legions along the Danube. In the East, the new, young Persian empire was flexing its muscles. The Christians were becoming so numerous and so brazenly contemptuous of the idea of the divinity of Caesar that an official persecution policy had to be instituted. While that did provide some opportunities for entertainment it also required personnel, which the emperors could scarcely spare in such times. More barbarians began appearing on more frontiers: Germans and Franks in Gaul and Germania; Goths and Visigoths and Alans in the Balkans and across Thrace and Asia Minor. And to make matters worse, the Roman-trained legions of colonial peoples, who had been given Roman citizenship (for what it was worth) in 212 and who had previously been faithful defenders of the frontiers, had learned the arts of politics and free enterprise and were now demanding cash or favors in return for their services.

Late in the third century the emperor Diocletian tried to deal with the gravest problem—the military pressures along the frontiers—by dividing the empire into halves, Eastern and Western, ruled by coequal emperors. All that accomplished was the creation of antagonistic courts, each eager to display its preeminence. Yet Diocletian's doctrine would not be undone until 312, when the Eastern Caesar, Constantine, invaded Italy and captured Rome. It took Constantine twelve years to suppress all the important opposition and officially reunite the empire under his sole rule. In those same dozen years Constantine made two decisions that must be counted among the most momentous decisions made by an individual in all history: he decided to become a Christian, and he decided to take his court away from Rome and build a new capital in the East.

The façade of the Pantheon (below) is undistinguished; it is as an interior that the structure is unsurpassed. The original temple to the seven planetary deities was constructed by Agrippa in 25 B.C. Hadrian rebuilt the structure in A.D. 120, adding a grand rotunda but retaining Agrippa's original portico (above). The dome itself (right, in an eighteenth-century painting by Pannini) is thought to date from an even later period, but a strong unity of design pervades the whole of the structure. The warm sunlight that bathes the Pantheon's interior is from a single source, an opening, twenty-seven feet in diameter, in the center of the coffered dome.

Constantine's conversion was not necessarily inevitable; nor was it, as it is sometimes suggested, necessarily opportunistic. Christians were numerous, but they were not powerful, and they were despised by much of the Roman ruling class. (Diocletian's brief claim of tolerance toward the Christians was so bitterly resisted in his own court that he reversed it with a declaration of persecution.) Constantine was a noted defender of Christians, probably because his mother, Helena, had chosen to become one. Before the Battle of the Milvian Bridge, during which he killed his rival Maxentius and thus gained Rome, Constantine claimed to have had a vision of a cross with the legend *In hoc signo vinces* above it. Clearly he was either already spiritually ready to convert or readying his court for a future announcement. The exact date of his conversion is not known, but it did occur before he had completed his unification efforts and thus entailed considerable political risk.

The empress Helena, incidentally, was a vigorous traveler and conscientious excavator; she is sometimes called the first archaeologist. After her son's victory near Rome, she went off to Jerusalem in search of Calvary and relics. When she located the probable Crucifixion site, she had built, at Constantine's direction, a shrine, the Church of the Holy Sepulcher. And in the church she placed the most sacred relic she had found—a piece of wood locally identified as having been part of the True Cross. The design of the Holy Sepulcher church was based on the central plan of—and domed like—the Pantheon.

In Rome itself, after Constantine's conversion and assumption of power, the Christians were able to leave the catacombs. A few wooden churches were built, mostly according to the old basilican plan, and Constantine himself commissioned a stone sanctuary for the city. Now known as St. Costanza, it was actually used as a mausoleum for the emperor's daughter Constantia; here, too, Constantine revealed his affection for the Pantheon-type central plan characterized by a cylindrical base and a dome. His preference would assume its greatest expression, however, in his new capital.

Constantine probably decided to build a new city because he realized that the empire was no longer strong enough to maintain its vast territory. Faithful troops were too few and available funds too limited to do much good spread out on two, three, or even four fronts. Since the barbarian threat was greatest in Western Europe, and since the empire's economic interests were greatest in the East—in Egypt, India, perhaps even with the temporarily antagonistic Persians—there was no question about which half of the empire was the more expendable. Besides, how would it look to the other Roman colonies if the capital city of the empire fell to barbarian invaders? Would not that eventuality encourage widespread insurrection? Better to move the capital to a more secure location, sparing no pomp in the process.

Constantine was a young man—only twenty-four at the time of his Milvian Bridge victory—filled with bold ideas and grand ambitions. True, he was willing to lose the Western colonies, but only because their maintenance was so costly; in addition, as Constantine saw it, wealth in the future would be determined by control of the trade routes to the East. He also saw the potential of the Christian religion as

Constantine's momentous decision to embrace Christianity was followed by an equally bold resolution to move his capital to the East. The earliest Christian churches followed Roman basilican plans, and Constantine himself (below, right) was partial to the Pantheon. The mausoleum he commissioned for his daughter Constantia (above) reveals his preference for a cylindrical base combined with a dome. The mausoleum was constructed in Rome in 330, shortly before Constantine moved his court to Byzantium. The ramparts and revetments that rose around his new capital (right) served as the bulwark of Christianity throughout the Middle Ages.

Overleaf: *The chief buildings erected in Constantine's new capital were churches for the new religion; the most outstanding of these is Hagia Sophia, Divine Wisdom.*

a unifier of peoples throughout the empire; and in 324 he tried to help it along by summoning the first worldwide ecumenical council of the Christian church. Of course he had to convene the council in Asia Minor, at Nicaea, mainly because of its central location (between Rome and the Holy Land) but also because he could not have held it at Rome. The political elders of Rome in their spiritual fatigue were reactionaries, cranky and suspicious. If Constantine was eager to revamp and reinvigorate the Roman Empire, the tired, old city of Rome was no place to begin.

He chose to begin at the site of the old Greek city of Byzantium, at the eastern tip of Thrace, overlooking the Bosporus, the narrow but vital waterway dividing two continents. To the north was the Black Sea and the great timber forests around it, and a rear entrance via the Danube into Eastern Europe; to the south was the Aegean world and the Mediterranean; and just across the way was Asia Minor, the threshold of the Orient. Even the geological formation of the site was ideal —hilly enough to provide an overview of the surrounding land and sea approaches and overlooking a crescent-shaped inlet that provided a fine protected harbor, the Golden Horn. And in 324, possibly while en route to or from the ecumenical council, Constantine stopped at Byzantium to make his decision official. The place was a virtual ruin, having lately been visited by marauding Goths. But that was all right with Constantine; he wanted to start from scratch. He set a stone in place and proclaimed the site the capital of the Christian Roman Empire. It was to be named Nea Roma, although almost no one ever called it that. From the time of its official dedication in 330, the new city was popularly known as the City of Constantine, Constantinople.

Constantine died in 337, and although he did not see his capital become a great booming metropolis, he did set the architectural tone of his city, and his successors followed his example as his predecessors in Rome had followed Augustus Caesar's example. In fact, there was a certain resemblance between Constantinople and Rome. The imperial forums provided the central civic meeting places; public baths were among the earliest works under construction; official business was conducted in the basilica; and a circus and theater complex called the Hippodrome was the primary entertainment center. Not surprisingly, where Rome had had temples, Constantinople had churches. It had one church in particular, a church so monumental and so magnificent that its reputation alone affected the development of European architecture for a thousand years.

The church called Hagia Sophia, or Divine Wisdom, was first built by Constantine as part of his initial plan for his new capital. Little is known about its appearance at its genesis, although it probably was modeled on the circular central plan of the Pantheon, to which Constantine was partial. A century later it was enlarged by Emperor Theodosius II, although the scope and the nature of his renovations are unknown. The Hagia Sophia with which we are familiar was begun in 532

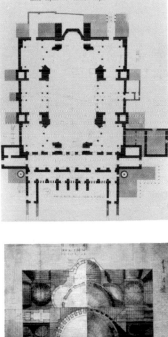

What the Parthenon is to ancient Greece, and the Pantheon to Rome, Hagia Sophia is to Byzantium. The prevailing motif of Byzantine architecture — the dome — is nowhere used to greater effect than here. Two semidomes (above) abut and buttress the grand central dome; the three form a canopy over a great oval nave (top) that is 225 feet long and 107 feet wide. The high minarets that ring Hagia Sophia's exterior (left) date from the fall of Constantinople to the Turks in 1453 and the church's conversion into a mosque. In 1934 it was again transformed, into a museum.

by order of Emperor Justinian and Empress Theodora, after the earlier sanctuary had been destroyed by fire. Astonishingly, although the new church was to be one of the largest and most structurally complex buildings in the world, such was the zeal on the part of the builders to finish it that it took a mere five years to erect.

The new Hagia Sophia had to be much bigger and many times grander than either of its predecessors, for it was, virtually by decree, the most important building in Constantinople. To serve in that capacity during the reign of Justinian and Theodora required far more scale and grandeur than had been required in the time of Constantine; in two centuries the city had come a long way. Originated as a rather literal new Rome, Constantinople promptly assumed a quality all its own. It was an imperial capital, it was a great seaport, and it was at the axis of a network of trade routes. Therefore it was something like Rome and Venice combined and a little like Alexandria or Damascus, too, which were neither Oriental nor Occidental but reflected something of the culture of both worlds.

By the Justinian era, the population of Constantinople was about 600,000, and the streets were like an international bazaar. No skin color was out of place, no foreign costume seemed eccentric; the sounds and smells and sights in the marketplace were exotic and familiar at the same time. In sixth-century Constantinople, one would not be surprised to meet a woman whose physical appearance suggested Celtic origins (which was altogether possible), wearing cosmetics from Egypt and a patterned wrap from Syria, who spoke only Greek and called herself Roman. Exposure to all the colorings, patternings, and motifs that decorated the abundance of goods made the people—and the builders—of the city inordinately sensitive to design, and their sensitivity was reflected in the construction of buildings. The city itself became sort of an international display piece.

The architectural formations were basically Greco-Roman—there was certainly no absence of colonnades and Roman arches—but the decoration testified to the international influences that were woven into the fabric of city life. Mosaics of bright-colored glazed and gilt tiles echoed the great mosaic traditions of Persia; a conspicuously growing tendency to cluster varisized domes reminded travelers of the architecture of India. Some of the decoration of foreign influence was not even picked up from architecture, but from other arts: masons in Constantinople sometimes carved stone—such as the marble on capitals—to resemble the finest Syrian lace. The introduction of these various elements into the architecture of Constantinople was a fairly rapid process, and by the time of Justinian and Theodora the distinctive Byzantine style, in all its full decorative lushness, was beginning to flourish. And flourish it did. All the old and new architectural formations that had been used at Constantinople, and all the parochial influences and traditions—architectural and otherwise—came together in a perfect blend at the church called Hagia Sophia.

From the outside Hagia Sophia looks every bit as massive and complex as it is. The exterior is not elaborately decorated, and so nothing distracts from the basic form, which is essentially symmetrical, rising in semidomed, modular steps to the great dome flanked by half domes over the center. It is an airy and beautiful structure, a gleaming weighty complex of varisized mounds, a monument that proclaims itself an engineering phenomenon. Inside its self-congratulatory proclamations cease. Inside there is only space—a great, high central space capped by a vast dome that has a ring-a-round of cutout arched windows; and around the central space are other spaces, recesses, all rounded at the tops and incised with arched light-giving openings.

Space and light are the main compositional elements of Hagia Sophia—as they are at the Pantheon—and the longer one stands inside the edifice, the more obvious that becomes. One sees the shape of the spaces between the arch-supporting columns of the elevation before one sees the arches and columns. Contributing to this effect are the carving on the stone—carving that makes the stone capitals or entablatures look like basket weave or lacework—and the hidden pendentives that invisibly support the great dome. In Hagia Sophia, moreover, light has conspicuous shape. It seems almost tangible as it pours in at different times, through different windows, strikes objects of its choice, and cre-

Although Justinian drove the Ostrogoths from Ravenna, the squat Mausoleum of Theodoric (right), greatest of the Ostrogothic kings, remains one of Ravenna's finest monuments. The church Justinian commissioned to commemorate Ravenna's recovery to the Byzantine Empire was St. Vitale (below, right). Its curious dome is constructed of earthen pots fitted into one another, the whole protected by a timber roof. Justinian also founded Ravenna's Church of St. Apollinaire in Classe (below). In the original mosaics above the altar, the saint preaches to his flock.

ates an ever-changing pattern of crisscrossing beams inside the vast interior. There are truly pillars of light, as real as the marble pillars that support the arches along the nave.

Originally the glitter and gleam of light in the edifice must have been far greater than they are now, for there were many more mosaics with the characteristically Byzantine abundance of gold. But Hagia Sophia is not what it was. Some of the mosaics may have been destroyed during the iconoclastic controversies that used to divide the Orthodox church. And everything Christian was removed in 1453, when Constantinople fell to Islam, and Hagia Sophia was converted into a mosque, complete with the added minarets. Today Hagia Sophia is a museum, and some of the mosaics long plastered over are being restored. But no change wrought by religion or politics has reduced the splendor of its great space volumes or the shapeliness of its dynamic lighting and so whatever restoration may be done—and no matter how welcome that restoration may be—it is only a restoration of detail, not of fundamentals.

Hagia Sophia was the first great architectural monument of the

Byzantine Empire, which, under Justinian, was almost as large and just about as powerful as the Roman Empire had been under Augustus. Justinian even managed to restore parts of the West to the empire, including all of Italy, although most of the restored territory split away again after his death. Nevertheless, through his successful expansion, the new Byzantine architecture characterized by Hagia Sophia moved into Southern and Eastern Europe. The Italian city of Ravenna remained a Byzantine outpost for centuries and was the home of one of the first major Byzantine structures outside of Constantinople: the Church of St. Vitale. Venice was never a Byzantine colony, but that prosperous city-state maintained close ties with Constantinople and was really rather similar in cosmopolitan composition and tastes. The Byzantine influence is apparent in the design of Venice itself, especially at the lavish, eleventh-century St. Mark's Basilica. Most real Byzantine architecture, however, was built at the direction of Constantinople in important colonial outposts. Most of the buildings were churches, many were quite exquisite, but none ever came close—in scale or grandeur or any other respect—to Hagia Sophia.

Hagia Sophia was much more than just the most important building in Constantinople; it was, in a very real sense, the queen church of Christendom. After all, the Byzantine Empire was the first Christian empire. Constantinople was the capital and the seat of the patriarch of the Orthodox church; and Hagia Sophia was the central church in the central city of the organized Christian world. That it was—and all in Byzantium were convinced of it—the most splendid building on earth was tangible proof of Christ's triumph. The cross ruled, and moreover it ruled from Constantinople.

There was some dissension, however. Almost from the start of the Christian religion, disagreements in theology developed between Latin-speaking and Greek-speaking Christians. These differences had managed to flourish even while all Christians were united by persecution and were forced to worship covertly. The first ecumenical council called by Constantine was in fact intended to deal with the schism. In the early centuries compromises were often worked out, and relations between East and West were cordial, with periodic breaches. But the overwhelming power of Christendom was centered in the East.

The West, meanwhile, was the scene of a gigantic panorama of human movement. Part migration, part invasion, the mobilizations had begun in late imperial times. Millions of people, mostly grouped into small tribes, poured across the Eurasian steppes and through the forests and down along the river valleys of the Romans' northern and western hinterland. There were just too many of them to deal with, and so Constantine had given up and gone to Byzantium. When the Roman legions disappeared, the tribes became hordes. They were Huns, Goths, Visigoths, Ostrogoths, Vandals, Burgundians, and Lombards, but the Romans, setting an example for later professional historians, lumped them all together and called them barbarians.

With no one but other barbarians to stop their advance, they overran the continent. In the year 410 the Visigoths under their chieftain Alaric laid siege to Rome. The siege was a success, and they celebrated

Alaric the Visigoth (above) sacked Rome in A.D. 410, the first of a wave of barbarian invasions that would plunge the Western Empire into centuries of darkness. In the East, the Iconoclasts wreaked another kind of destruction—the breaking of idols and images. In the manuscript illustration below, an image of Christ is being obliterated.

Overleaf: The Byzantine artists and craftsmen whose work was proscribed by the Iconoclasts fled to Italy. Their talents are particularly apparent in this Canaletto painting of St. Mark's in Venice.

with three days of sacking; when they left, little remained of Rome. The Visigoths went on to settle Spain, abandoning the Italian peninsula to the next visitors, the Vandals. Led by Gaiseric, they "vandalized" the little that was left of Rome in 455. Then came the turn of the Ostrogoths, who had the misfortune of being the occupiers of Italy when Emperor Justinian decided to restore Italy to the empire. The Byzantine legions drove the Ostrogoths across the Alps and apparently into oblivion. Three years after Justinian's death in 565, the Lombards invaded the peninsula, but they were more careful than their predecessors; they did not occupy Rome, Naples, Ravenna, and most of the eastern coastlands, thus leaving unthreatened those areas closest to the Byzantine heart. The strategy worked; the powerful armies of Constantinople did not interfere.

Italy, of course, was only part of the panorama. Indeed, the picture in Italy was probably less bleak than it was elsewhere. Rome might be sacked, but too much remained of the trappings of a great ancient culture to be wiped out entirely. In addition, the Byzantine influence remained in Italy; Ravenna and to some extent Venice bore evidence of a living, thriving culture.

Elsewhere the barbarian invasions drew a cloak over whatever cultural progress the Roman Empire had brought to the peoples of the West. The growth of literacy, the development of art, and the advancement of law all but stopped in the West between the first sacking of Rome and the rise of Charlemagne. True, whole new nations were taking embryonic shape; true, the foundation of a whole new civilization was being laid. But the embryo was gestating and the foundation being dug in dark ages.

But even in the darkness, Western Christians continued to go their own way. The Latin fathers were developing a religion very different from that of the East. Monasticism appeared before the fifth century. Shortly thereafter, Augustine formally founded a Western theology, based on Classical philosophy. The idea of an almost monarchical pope, bearer of the apostolic tradition, was a constant source of discussion and definition. Hagia Sophia did not serve as a monument to this kind of Christianity; the great Church of Hagia Sophia, to the Latin fathers, symbolized the opposition.

Constantinople did not really care what Rome thought, as long as Rome committed no heresy and Constantinople held all the power. And after the sackings of the fifth century, the future of Rome looked doubtful anyway. The invaders had driven away or killed much of the population, and the destruction of the aqueducts made the city all but uninhabitable—after the second sacking, only fifty thousand people remained, a loss of about half a million. Moreover, the decay of Rome continued through the sixth, seventh, and eighth centuries; the Latin fathers still convened there, but prelates in Constantinople could hardly have felt threatened.

There were, however, two events during the West's Dark Ages that insured the future independence and eventual equality of the Latin church. One was the barbarian conversions, and the other was the rise of Islam.

In 496 a Frankish king, Clovis, became a Christian. He may have been the first of the barbarian chieftains to convert, but he was by no means the last. For the barbarian invaders had cultural aspirations. They might loot a vanquished city dry, but the booty they carried off, they were bound to realize, was better than anything they could make. They might level a stone temple, but it could not have taken them too long to admit that a stone building was something they themselves could not build. The Romans had art and architecture, laws and language, and the Christian religion. If the conquerors were to be the new Romans, then they must have those things. It would require a couple of centuries to learn to build with stone, a couple of generations to learn to read and write, but religion they could have at once—and give to their people by decree.

In 622 the Prophet Mohammed declared the existence of the nation of Islam; within ten years the religion he had founded had enveloped the Arabian peninsula. By 644 the Arab legions, bent on expanding the religion through conquest, had overrun Syria, Persia, and Egypt. The Moslem advance was astonishing. By mid-century the Byzantine Empire had lost all of its Asian and African territory except Asia Minor to Islam; the Holy Land was in Moslem hands; and in 673 a Moslem fleet arrived at the Bosporus, instituted a blockade of Constantinople itself, and laid siege. The siege failed, but the blockade and siege became an annual enterprise for five years. Islam had appeared from nowhere, and nothing would ever be the same for Byzantium again. Its supremacy over the Mediterranean world suddenly gone, Constantinople now had good cause to fear for its own life. Help was needed, and the only place to find help was among other Christians. Theological differences were not erased overnight—in some ways the disagreements grew worse—but after 680 Constantinople finally recognized Rome as an equal partner in Christendom, and no longer as a wayward delinquent that would someday be brought under the proprietary cape of the patriarch.

When the Frankish king Charlemagne crowned himself regent of a new Roman Empire in 800, he ended, for all intents and purposes, the Dark Ages. But the unity he achieved was fragile and artificial, and it died with him. Then the more realistic, more natural product of the previous four centuries' history took shape. The product was European civilization, a world united up to a point by Roman Catholicism, but divisible into individual nations, each one defined by the more or less common language spoken by its inhabitants. They were not yet Germans, Frenchmen, Italians, and so forth; but no longer were they lumped together as barbarians.

No doubt Charlemagne would have loved nothing more than to see a Western Hagia Sophia rising over Rome or Paris. He certainly tried, during his brief regency, to institute a revival of Classical learning within the empire. And it is documented that the emperor assembled artists and craftsmen from Constantinople to teach Westerners the more refined Eastern trades. To build his own tomb and chapel he imported materials and masons from the Byzantine city of Ravenna; the handsome result, not surprisingly, is a Byzantine building, the Palatine

Long after the Byzantine Empire had fallen, its spirit lived on —particularly in the wooden churches of Russia and Northern Europe. The wooden church of Borgund (above) dates from the thirteenth century and reflects motifs that reach their highest expression in the rainbow-hued domes of the Church of St. Basil the Blessed (right) in Moscow.

The Palatine Chapel of Aachen (left), built by Charlemagne as a mausoleum, bears a striking resemblance to St. Vitale—and indeed, Charlemagne imported both masons and materials from Ravenna. The chapel's interior (above) is capped by a dome.

Chapel at Aachen. It is a dignified structure, with heavier walls and less spaciousness than most Byzantine architecture (probably an accommodation to the cooler northern climate), but it is not Hagia Sophia.

Indeed, the stone-building art came slowly to the West. But it did come, and once started, it was hard to stop. Western Christendom needed churches, and after the year 1000 it began to get them. Their style was named—much later—Romanesque, or "in the Roman manner," and for good reason. The churches have basilican plans—rectangular, with long naves enclosed by columns and flanked by aisles—and

The Romanesque was a learning style, a century of transition marked by considerable trial and error. Decoration was most often minimal, but sometimes, as in St. Michael's in Hildesheim (below), the more exuberant barbarian motifs came into play. Pisa Cathedral (left), known for its famous leaning campanile, has a typically Romanesque basilican plan. However the church's transepts with an apse at each end mark an important step forward. Laach Abbey (right), where the vaulting bays of naves and aisles are of the same width, represents another progression toward the Gothic.

unadorned columns support round arches. But there is really no Roman spirit here, no molded spaces and dramatically juxtaposed shapes. It is, at first, just what it must be—a strong, sober, learning style, self-conscious and transitional. Sometimes—as at St. Michael's in Hildesheim—there are touches of the old geometric barbarian decorative motifs, but more often there is no decoration, or just Byzantine-derived decoration. The columns are cylindrical, fat and plain; the early ceilings are flat, but soon give way to the barrel vault over the nave.

Then something happened, strangely enough in France, early in the twelfth century. The actual dimensions of the churches did not change immediately, but the builders began trying to make the dimensions look different. Fat, round columns were replaced by clusters of slender planks and cylinders called piers because clustered piers give a greater appearance of height. The arches along the aisles were raised—more space, less stone, also to give the illusion of height. Windows were enlarged; more light was wanted as well as more height. The builders were trying to complete the transition.

The following is an entirely probable fantasy. A monk, robust, cheerful, intelligent, is walking in his monastery garden near Paris and hears horses coming down the road; it is 1150. He hurries to the roadside to see half a dozen knights, dust-covered and obviously tired, approach. Waving at them to stop, he asks if they would like rest and refreshment, and they are grateful. After they have cleaned up, he sits with them as they eat. Were they Crusaders? he inquires. They say yes, and there is a moment's sympathetic reflection on the ill-fated Second Crusade, aborted the previous year without even reaching the Holy Land. Did they, however, at least get to see Constantinople? Yes, they did. And then, did they visit the celebrated Hagia Sophia? Indeed they did, and what a vision it was. He listens as they describe its glories, and when they are through eating and drinking and praising the great Eastern edifice, the monk asks the knights if they will do him the kindness

of following him. He leads them to the abbey church, which was built just a few years earlier. The abbé himself had designed the church—in fact, he had himself selected the timbers from the nearby wood and the stone from the quarry—and he feels that it is a rather unusual church. The knights are impressed. Never in France had they seen so light and airy a sanctuary; the piers are high and slender, and the arches over the ribbed vault are pointed instead of round. All the arches are pointed and quite high, and the windows are much larger than usual. It is almost as if this church has no walls at all, but is a frame of stone and timber. The light pours into every nook and cranny, bathing the whole interior in its warmth.

The Church of La Madeleine at Vézelay (left) has a typically Romanesque barrel-vaulted nave; but the brightly lighted choir beyond with its pointed arches and vaults is Gothic. St. Sernin's (above) in Toulouse is a Romanesque structure, though the church's central octagonal tower is clearly Gothic. It is the Abbey Church of Saint-Denis (right) whose unity of design, combining the essential elements of light and height, gives the edifice the distinction of being the first truly Gothic building.

The knights are generous in their praise. But, the monk asks somewhat hesitantly, how does this church compare with Hagia Sophia? Well, the chivalrous knights reply at once, this church certainly compares favorably with Hagia Sophia. The monk is so obviously skeptical that one of the knights, with a gift of metaphor, volunteers the truth. Hagia Sophia, he says, is like a queen at court, wearing a golden crown and a cape encrusted with jewels; this church is a little girl on the edge of a wood, wearing a white gown and one perfect gem.

Abbé Suger escorts his guests back to their horses and watches them depart, thinking about the now-finished holy war. While they were away, following King Louis VII, he, Suger, had been entrusted with the government of France. Now that Louis is back, he is just what he best likes being—the abbé of Saint-Denis monastery. He walks to the new abbey church again and considers the knight's metaphor. He decides that it pleases him—he did not really think his church was the equal of Hagia Sophia, did he?—and the inventor of the architecture called Gothic smiles.

5

The Cathedral Crusade

As a series of military enterprises, the Crusades were something of a sham. Ostensibly their goal was the expulsion of the infidel Moslems from the Holy Land and its permanent restoration to Christendom. To the extent that the professed goal was achieved, the First Crusade was the only successful one. In 1099, only four years after Pope Urban II had launched the sacred war of liberation with the cry of "God wills it!" a huge Christian army marched into Jerusalem and returned the holy city to the rule of the Cross. In 1187, Jerusalem was retaken by the Moslems. Altogether eight Crusades were declared during a period of less than two hundred years; half of them were unmitigated fiascos; none of them regained Jerusalem for Christendom for any substantial length of time.

But the Crusades were much more than a series of military enterprises. They were a rare cultural phenomenon, a camouflaged vehicle for affecting dramatic social, political, and economic changes in the world. In both Christendom and Islam, for example, the Crusades were responsible for shifting the center of power from the older, traditional leadership to the younger, more ambitious elements of the civilization. When the holy wars began, Christendom was dominated by the Easterners, possessors of the Greco-Roman cultural traditions; and Islam was still under the strong influence of Arabic leadership, the inheritor of the legacy of the ancient Persian and Egyptian civilizations. When the Crusades were over the Christian world was centered in the West, and its wealth and might resided in the hands of Norman, Frankish, and Germanic kings and bishops—hands that had only a few hundred years before wielded the battle-axes of barbarianism. Islam was dominated by the Seljuk Turks, relatively recent arrivals from the Asian no-man's-land north of Persia—known as Sogdiana—a people of Mongolian descent who had converted from their nature-worshiping paganism to Islam as recently as the tenth century.

The Crusades, then, were struggles within struggles, and they produced big winners and big losers on both sides. Moreover, particularly in the West, the Crusades provided the means by which a whole society could convert itself from the feudal agrarian system that had characterized the early Middle Ages to an urban mercantile system. The eleventh century in Western Europe had seen the land devastated by wars, blight, and plague. People were uprooted by the thousands,

The building boom sparked by Abbé Suger's Gothic church at Saint-Denis is illustrated in the 1448 illumination detail at left. Although only eight are visible, twelve churches, each honoring one of the apostles, are shown in different stages of construction.

precipitating mass migration. The First Crusade channeled the migration and gave purpose to the movement; the great mass pilgrimage to the East established a new network of routes and a system of way stations that would serve as trade routes when the time came. The later Crusades also demonstrated to the Westerners that they had stiff competition to meet if they were to prosper as traders in the international marketplace, for Constantinople had a strategic location and centuries of experience to its advantage. In the Fourth Crusade the competition was dealt with. The Holy Land forgotten, the Westerners invaded Constantinople in 1204, drove out the Byzantine leadership, sacked and gutted the city, and on its ruins declared the Latin Empire of the East.

Perhaps the greatest change affected by the Crusades was on the mentality of the Westerners. More than any other event the Crusades created a sense of collective purpose in the minds of the people. Nationalism had never developed in Europe because nations had never lasted long; furthermore, feudalism was not a system that fostered a sense of nationhood. The Crusaders were joined not only by common goals, but by common experience. When the Westerners arrived at Constantinople en route to the Holy Land, they shared a feeling of awe and intimidation and a realization of cold, hard fact. The many journals kept by literate Crusaders record the same culture shock. There is Constantinople; that is a city; there is nothing like that at home. That is Hagia Sophia; surely it was built by the hand of God Himself; there is nothing like that at home. Journalistic descriptions of Jerusalem were respectful and pious, but the written descriptions of Constantinople were like the descriptions of the heavily laden table at a regal banquet by men who were starving.

It is not surprising, then, that after 1100 the church builders of France began to experiment with new architectural forms that would make their churches look higher and lighter. The First Crusade, almost entirely a Norman and Frankish enterprise, had exposed the Westerners to their own artistic backwardness. The generation that had liberated Jerusalem had also seen Hagia Sophia; they brought home the news. The builders did what they could.

Abbé Suger of Saint-Denis made the first breakthrough; then the crusading spirit took over. The rallying cry of the First Crusade—"God wills it!"—served the bishops of France well in the twelfth century. The will of God seemed to be the force behind their every act. Surely God had willed the unprecedented political power then concentrated in the Church; God's will undoubtedly was responsible for the astonishingly rapid growth of the towns; God must will a suitable new edifice to serve the spiritual needs of a growing population and to proclaim His sovereignty over the diocese; God would will a tax to pay for it.

There was one nagging question about God's will. Could it be assumed that God willed such grand monuments as Hagia Sophia for every town? Hagia Sophia was, after all, an Eastern church, and the East had different ideas from the West about the will of God.

The most influential theologian in twelfth-century France was Abbé Bernard of Clairvaux (later, Saint Bernard), a good friend to Abbé Suger of Saint-Denis. Bernard was an advocate of simplicity, aus-

Little remains of the Abbey Church of Cluny (above), but when it was completed in 1131 (top in a period engraving) its 443-foot nave and choir were the longest in France. Innovative —and influential—it had one of the earliest examples of the pointed arch and changed the course of church design in France. Among its many descendants is the great cathedral at Le Mans (right).

terity, humility; he had an opinion on everything, and his opinions carried great weight. When the abbey church at Cluny was nearing completion around 1130, the abbé of Clairvaux condemned the structure as too ostentatious to be compatible with monastic humility, citing in particular the "immense" height, "immoderate" length, and "supervacuous" width and calling for the removal of the "monstrous" Romanesque figure carving within. Not much remains of Cluny today, but we do know that it was expressive of the sort of monumentality that builders had been seeking in their quest for a rival to Hagia Sophia. The church had double aisles and double transepts, a high barrel vault over the nave, and was probably the first European building with pointed arches in the nave arcade. In other words, the Cluniac church was innovative and monumental: was anything innovative and monumental going to be humble enough to be acceptable to this latter-day disciple of Saint Augustine?

No one knew for sure, and it did matter. Bernard was influential enough to regulate the pace and shape of building throughout France. He was not necessarily personally vindictive or stubborn, but the fact was that money for a building endorsed by the abbé would flow from aristocratic sources more freely than for a building of eccentric style.

The one person who did not worry too much about Bernard was Abbé Suger. In his time Suger had been the second most powerful man in France, second only to the king he advised, and now he was old and wanted to build his new abbey church. He had raised most of the money and even assembled some of the materials in the late 1120's, but he would not begin until he had worked out a design that pleased him. He probably considered Bernard's ideas, and may have agreed that ostentation had no place in a church. On the other hand, the notion of equating austerity with humility did not sit well with the abbé of Saint-Denis. Certainly a man felt humble seated in a bare, undecorated cell, but could he not also feel humble walking through a field of

Abbé Suger described his church as "pervaded by a wonderful and continuous light entering through the most sacred windows." Light does indeed suffuse the interior of Saint-Denis (left), radiating through Suger's "sacred windows" of stained glass. Although such glass was not unknown before the building of Saint-Denis, the abbey church marks the first time it was used on such a grand scale. Other treasures of Saint-Denis include the priceless serpentine paten above. The anachronistic fifteenth-century illumination at right depicts the seventh-century rebuilding of Saint-Denis in the Gothic style.

flowers, warmed by the sun, entertained by songbirds? Had not Saint Augustine said that Christ was, literally, the Divine Light? Even Bernard believed that light was the earthly presence closest in substance to God. Did not the presence of God make a man feel humble? What, then, was so special about a small, dark church? Why not a bright church? Why not a church filled with the presence, the very substance of God? Why not a high, open church with polished floors, gleaming white stone figures, soaring arches, and burnished woods to reflect the light? Why not indeed.

Gothic architecture is not an evolutionary extension of the Romanesque. By 1140, when Suger finally began to construct his abbey church, several churches in France had the familiar pointed arches and groin vaulting that are so closely associated with the Gothic, but they were not Gothic. Furthermore, the third familiar architectural feature of the Gothic—flying buttresses—is not employed at Saint-Denis at all. Nevertheless, Saint-Denis is the first Gothic building. It holds that distinction because it has the unity of design and the particular light-letting properties that are essential to the style. The church was dedicated in 1144. Even Bernard of Clairvaux was able to accept the new kind of building, and the cathedral crusade that God willed got under way.

As soon as the workmen finished at Saint-Denis, they were employed by the bishop of Sens to build a great new cathedral in the *style ogivale*, or "pointed style," as the French called it. (The term "Gothic" was given to the architecture by the Italian Renaissance historian Giorgio Vasari, who disliked the style and named it for the barbarians he suggested might have originated it—although he must have known better.) Within ten or twelve years funds were being raised by the bishops of Paris, Le Mans, and Laon. Before the end of the century, grand new cathedrals were also under construction at Soissons, Bourges, and Chartres—the one at Chartres replaced one of the world's oldest churches, which had burned down in 1194. Early in the thirteenth century, the contagion spread to Reims, Amiens, Rouen, Beauvais, and Strasbourg. Then on it went, extending into Flanders and Germany and across the channel to England, making inroads into Spain and even skeptical Italy.

So much variation is possible in the design and construction of a Gothic cathedral that it is impossible to describe one and call it typical of all. The individuality of the edifices really is quite remarkable, for it developed in an era of rigid attitudes, when uniformity was sought in all aspects of life, when departure from prescribed procedure could be and often was considered heresy, when improvisation was suspect. Nevertheless, although the cathedral builders used common elements and applied common structural principles, they were permitted enormous leeway. The elements and principles were means; the end was the particular aura that itself is the main characteristic of the Gothic. An aura can hardly be defined, much less standardized, and to achieve it the builders could manipulate the means as they saw fit.

The Cathedral of Notre-Dame de Chartres, however, is a fitting subject for a brief description of a Gothic cathedral. (Because of its fame and the fame of its host city, the Paris cathedral usually comes to mind when one hears the name "Notre-Dame." Actually almost all French cathedrals are dedicated to Our Lady and are properly called "Notre-Dame," but like Chartres, they are more commonly referred to simply by the names of the towns where they are situated.) Although it is no more typical of the Gothic than any other single cathedral, Chartres has a structural simplicity and an uncomplicated layout that make it easier to discuss and analyze than many other cathedrals. This is the sole reason for its inclusion here; cathedrals in the Gothic style that differ from it should not be regarded as atypical or less pure examples of the Gothic.

The Cathedral of Chartres is laid out in the medieval version of the ancient Roman basilican plan (see diagram, page 89). It is a cross-shaped plan, rounded at the end of its longer member. This semicircular protrusion, beyond the intersection of the members, is called the apse. The innermost section of the apse, also semicircular, is the choir, where the altar is located. Behind the choir is a circular corridor, the ambulatory, and off the ambulatory is a series of small chapels. The longest section of the cross is occupied by the nave, where the worshipers congregate, and the nave is flanked by aisles. The shorter member of the cross, the member that is perpendicular to the nave, is

The cathedral-building contagion spread to Amiens in 1220, when the nave of that city's cathedral was begun. Amiens' western façade (below) is one of the finest in France, with serried statues resembling those at Notre-Dame de Paris. The interior (right) boasts wonderfully carved wooden choir stalls.

The transept and the area where the nave and transept intersect is appropriately called the crossing.

Like all Gothic churches, Chartres is primarily a vertical structure designed from the inside out. Thus the layout of the Gothic structure is, in a way, much less important than the layout of a Classical building. Inasmuch as Classical architecture was a blend of horizontal and vertical elements, the floor plan was parallel to the roof and therefore dictated the shape of interior volumes. The Gothic floor plan influenced the function of interior spaces, but not their shapes, which were determined by the vertical elements.

The primary vertical element in the Gothic cathedral was the pier, a cluster of slender pillars. A double row of piers defined the nave and separated it from the aisles. If lines were drawn on the floor from one pier base to the one opposite it across the nave and to the piers flanking it in the same row, the whole layout would be divided into rectangles. The lines in fact do not exist, but the rectangular forms do, and they are called bays. Each bay was roofed by a network of six arches that formed the groined vault. Two of the arches were round and intersecting; each extended from the top of a pier diagonally across the bay to the top of its corresponding pier on the other side of the nave. Arches were also constructed between piers directly opposite one another on the four corners of the bay. Because the diagonal of a square or rectangle is longer than the distance from corner to corner, the corner-to-corner arches, if they were round, would not rise as high as the diagonal arches. Therefore, the four arches over the sides of the bay were extended upward at the middle and pointed to reach the height of the two intersecting diagonal round arches.

Another row of shorter piers was built at the outside of each aisle. These piers were only about half the height of the nave piers, but they, too, were vaulted. The high-vaulted nave arches and the lower aisle arches, with the piers supporting them, formed the skeleton of the Gothic cathedral. The skeleton is completely exposed, and according to the aesthetics favored by builders in the period, especially in the earlier years, the less added to conceal the skeleton, the better. That is why Chartres has always been a favorite among scholars and architects; its skeleton is clearly visible and uncluttered with superfluous detail.

But since the cathedral did have to be enclosed somehow, such interferences as roofs and walls had to be added. At Chartres the elevation rose in three levels. The first rose to the height of the aisle vaults, and from the top of the arcade level to the top of the outermost walls a platform of timber was built. The second level of the arcade at Chartres is only fourteen feet high and is called the triforum. Timber was extended from the top of the triforum level to the top of the outer walls, where it was joined with the platform, forming a triangular passageway within the church over the aisles and roofing the aisles. The rest of the elevated nave vault, the clerestory, was windowed.

For builders, vaulted construction had always created a problem not present in post-and-lintel construction. In the latter, the weight of horizontal members bears directly down on the supporting vertical members; it might be said that the walls and columns hold the ceiling up,

The Cathedral of Chartres was rebuilt in only twenty-seven years, after a catastrophic fire in 1194 gutted an earlier structure. The plan of Chartres (below) is characterized by a short nave and an unusual choir whose shape was determined by the crypt of the older church. Chartres' world-famous western façade (left) is dominated by two asymmetrical spires; the northern one a marvel of the High Gothic, the other earlier one, severe and restrained. A portion of the cathedral's renowned sculpture can be seen in the south porch (above).

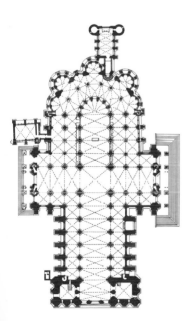

and the ceiling presses the walls and columns down. A vault, however, creates a downward and outward force on the vertical elements; the arches tend to push the supporting columns outward. This force is called thrust. When successive arches are built over a colonnade, the thrust of one arch is counterbalanced by the thrust of the adjacent arch, and the supporting column or pier receives its necessary downward strength. The problem comes at the extremes. The final columns in the row or the outer walls have no counterbalancing force, and if they fall, then the domino theory goes to work. The Romans and the builders of Romanesque churches had little trouble dealing with the problem: they simply built supporting verticals, called buttresses, against the outermost walls. In Gothic building, however, the higher nave vaults soared high above the height of the outer walls, and the thrust of the central vault was not countered with the buttresses flanking the aisle walls. The problem was solved first at Notre-Dame de Paris, and the solution soon became a familiar feature of Gothic architecture. It was the flying buttress, an arched support that extended from the standard vertical buttress of the lower walls in a gentle curve to the outside of the clerestory.

Building booms are not unusual in history. In our own time, between 1950 and 1970, many of the world's cities have been transformed, or at the least altered, by an astonishing quantity of construction. But the more one reflects on the cathedral crusade, the more remarkable the phenomenon seems. Cathedrals were not financed by banks; they were paid for by the communities that built them. The Church, it is true, had wide powers to tax, but medieval times were not prosperous times, and even with taxes at their highest, there was a limited surplus after the expenses of operating the diocese were met. Most of the cost had to come from private donations. The local aristocracy might be good for an annual donation, but the brunt had to be borne by the middle and working classes. The merchants were generally eager to contribute, for to them a great cathedral was a business investment. "The temple has always attracted the merchant just because it attracts the faithful . . . ," a medieval chronicler wrote. "There is no feast without its fair, no fair without its feast: one calls for the other."

The craftsmen often had their services to donate, and they, too, were willing; for the building of a cathedral, which could take years, kept a town bustling and the workbench busy. In the town of Chartres, where the local people had long carried on a deep-seated love affair with their cathedral, each of the local guilds paid for one of the edifice's magnificent stained-glass windows, and its contribution was recorded graphically in a smaller stained-glass window beneath the contribution. There is a great arched window telling the story of Saint Martin, and below is a small square window picturing a cobbler at his bench. The bishop of Laon had to implore the farmers and vintners of his diocese to increase their donations so that work on his fine cathedral could continue. They agreed, but exacted a price—immortality in stone. On the towers at Laon are carvings of oxen, and on the column capitals are carved grapevines. Oddities abound from one cathedral to another, but the cathedrals were built.

The intricate silver and gilt reliquary above, in the shape of a Gothic cathedral, is one of the treasures of the Church of St. Taurin in Evreux. With its gemlike stained glass and delicate stone tracery, the rose window at right is surely one of the treasures of Notre-Dame de Paris. Built by Jean de Chelles in about 1250, it graces the cathedral's northern façade.

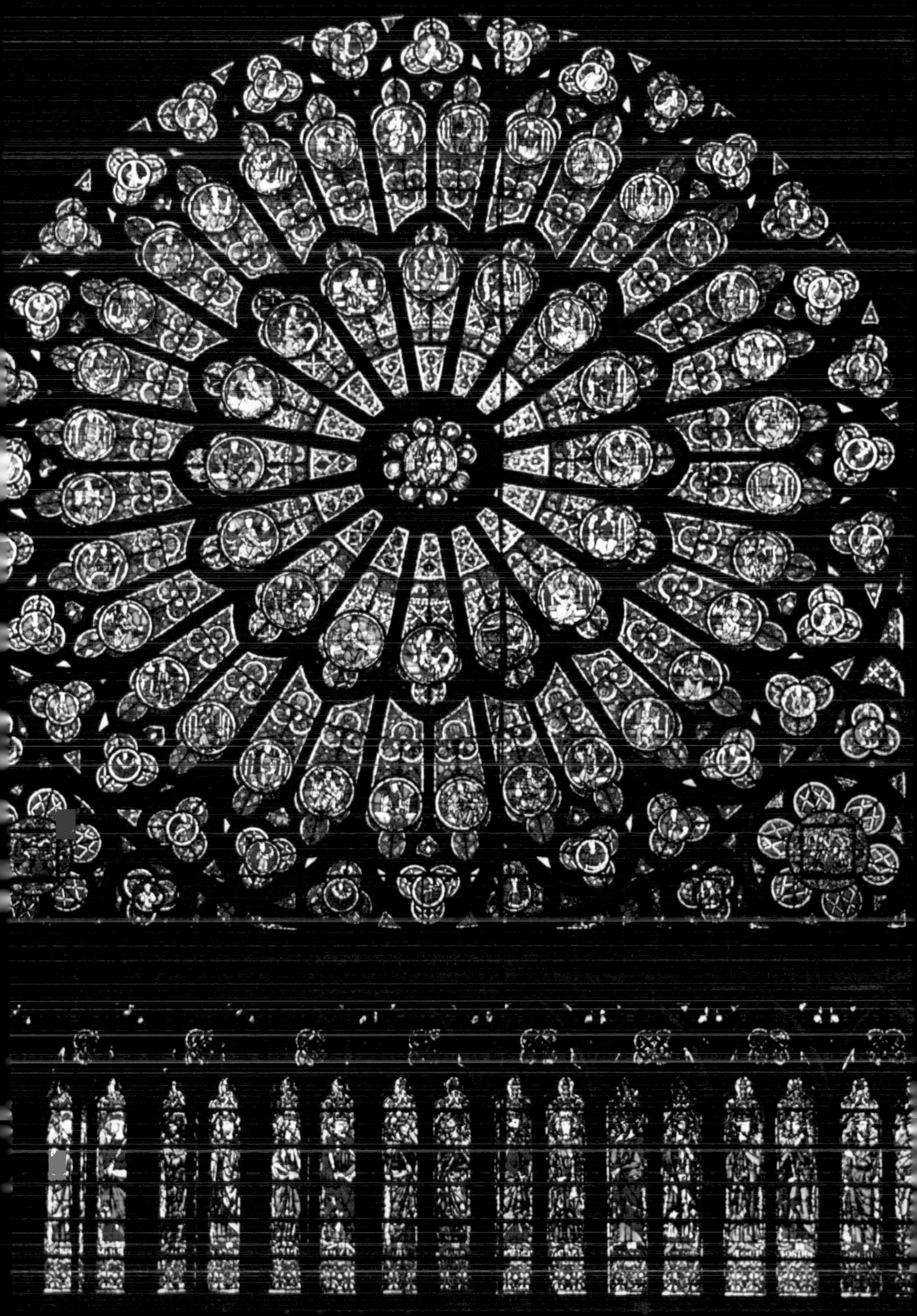

If the truth be told, though, the bishops of France had created their Frankenstein. The Church had always been extremely powerful in medieval Europe. In feudal times, however—and it should be noted that the feudal system in France had begun to wane in the eleventh century —there had been an informal sort of check and balance between the powers of the clerical and the secular sectors. The lords of the manors and the bishops, who exercised different responsibilities in the same region, jealously guarded their own prerogatives and kept one another if not exactly honest, at least on the right side of excess. Logically, the sudden and swift growth of communes and towns after 1100 should have destroyed the balance of power to the advantage of the bishops. The power of the lord or baron was based on his ownership of land and on his right to claim a percentage of the crops grown on his land. The power of the bishop was based on the right of the Church, under the system called mortmain, to collect taxes on the goods produced in the diocese. It made no difference to the bishop whether he was taxing farm goods or manufactured goods. When the agrarianism of the early Middle Ages changed to mercantilism in the twelfth century, the bishop's comparative power grew because the lord's dwindled. Moreover, the bishop traditionally was a town figure simply because the cathedral, the seat of the diocese, was usually situated in a town and, unless the town was quite large, functioned as a sort of town center. The rise of the towns, then, was concurrent with the rise of the bishops' power. And what better way to broadcast this new power than by building a great cathedral?

Ironically, the means used to broadcast the Church's power also ultimately subverted that power. The cathedrals were very, very expensive. In exchange for donations of labor and money from the middle class, the bishops had to permit the cathedral to be used for community purposes: political assemblies, theater, festivals, and guild meetings. Actually the cathedral as a community center was a fine idea and worked well in most towns. But given the constitution of the medieval Church, which buckled a bit every time a secular institution was strengthened, it was ultimately self-destructive.

The thirteenth-century Cathedral of Reims was one of the most elaborate in France, and the bishop of Reims wanted it completed quickly. Reims was a great producer of linens, and the bishop had long been collecting a high tax on the profits of the weavers' and linen merchants' commune. He also had been collecting a tariff on all exported goods, which in the case of Reims meant linens. Thus the commune had been fuming over the double tax on the same merchandise for years. But in the Middle Ages resistance to a bishop was not even easy to contemplate. At one point, however, the Reims commune was asked by a brother commune in Auxerre for a substantial loan, and Reims agreed. But as the chest of money was about to be transported to Auxerre, the bishop's agent informed the commune that the chest of money constituted an exportable item and that under mortmain the bishop was entitled to his percentage. Middle Ages or no, the commune resisted. It even refused to pay its normal taxes until the bishop withdrew his demand. The bishop responded by announcing that he would use force to collect the taxes. The weavers responded by seizing the local military compound, killing the bishop's agent, arming themselves, storming the cathedral building site, removing enough timber and stone to build barricades in the streets, and settling in for battle. The bishop said with some alacrity that it had all been a misunderstanding and backed down, his demands withdrawn.

The bishops were in something of a bind. In the twelfth century, the old-school, absolutist bishop of Laon imposed terrific taxes on the diocese. Some local burghers sent a delegation to inform His Grace that they and the serfs on the farms were starving to death. That, they were told, was their problem. So the burghers and the serfs joined together, invaded the cathedral, burned it, and killed several priests and the bishop. His successor, incidentally, was the bishop who—gladly—permitted the oxen figures and grapevine carving to be included in the new cathedral. In fact, the new bishop was so conciliatory that with the enthusiastic help of a cooperative population, the cathedral begun in 1160 was usable after only twelve years. Yet, clearly, the cooperation was achieved at the expense of Church authority.

At about the time their cathedral was nearing completion, the people of Laon instituted an annual celebration for which they became famous: the Feast of Fools. The day was given over to a vicious public mockery of the Church hierarchy. The presiding officer was the "pope"—the town idiot. The "archbishops" and "bishops"—local dunces and beggars—celebrated a boisterous, lewd Mass. After gorging themselves with food and drink, the participants concluded with the

Reims Cathedral (above, left) served as the coronation church of the kings of France and largely inspired the design of Westminster Abbey. Gothic cathedral design was also to influence other art forms, as is illustrated by the pointed arches included in the thirteenth-century ivory diptych (above) depicting Christ's Passion.

Overleaf: *The delicate flying buttresses, the soaring fleche, and, beyond, the two western towers of Notre-Dame de Paris rise in unfettered splendor on the banks of the Seine.*

Procession of the Ragamuffins—patterned after the processions of the high clergy. Then the local folk bombarded the proxy hierarchy with rotten fruits and vegetables and went home.

If the Feast of Fools was abuse by proxy, the abusiveness of the medieval mason toward the bishop was direct, day in and day out. Indeed, no aspect of the cathedral crusade better illustrates the ultimately subversive nature of that enterprise than the rise of the mason. For the rise of the mason was a symptom of the rise of secularism, and it was secularism, after all, that subverted not only the power of the Church but the medieval way of life.

When church building began in earnest in the West, in the eleventh century, the mason was usually a "working brother"—that is, a skilled worker, more often than not illiterate—attached to a monastery. The designer, such as he was, of buildings was generally a monk or nobleman, and the mason was approximately the equivalent of a construction foreman. But as building slowly became more sophisticated and the decorative challenges greater, a simple fact of life began to assert itself on the mason—and began to cut away some of the underpinnings of medieval assumptions. Consider this example. While the Abbey Church of Saint-Denis was under construction, Abbé Suger was visited by his friend Bishop Geoffrey of Chartres. At that time Geoffrey was about to begin construction of a new west portal at Chartres, and he was examining the stonework at Saint-Denis. The work of a certain carver particularly impressed the bishop, and he asked Suger to see to it that that mason was assigned to Chartres as soon as he was finished at the monastery. Now consider what that request must have meant to the cutter. Medieval art, like medieval life, was valued for its uniformity. Innovations in art were as unwelcome as nonconformity in life-style. There were conventions for every sort of depiction in stonecarving. The obedient mason simply followed the rules. But that did not mean that every carver carved alike. The carver singled out by Bishop Geoffrey had a special talent, some distinguishable facility that set his work apart. And if his work was special, he was special.

By that time, most masons and stonecutters were no longer forced laborers, but independent workingmen available for hire. And as the cathedral crusade began, certain masons and cutters found themselves and their services in demand in a number of places. He might still be illiterate, he might still be a pauper, but the sought-after mason knew he was unique. And once he knew that, he knew that he had power.

At first, the masons asserted themselves slowly. Their initial request seemed modest enough, and it was granted. It may have been the most far-reaching concession ever won in labor negotiations—the masons' lodge. At every building site in France, the bishops agreed, a long, one-storied structure would be built. Inside the lodge were compartments for preparing stones and storing tools, for napping and dining. The lodge was important because it gave the masons a place to protect their tools from weathering and theft, but it was much more important as a place where a mason could retire with his colleagues, to talk shop and share complaints. Because of it the masons of Europe were able to form a true brotherhood, to strengthen their organization, to achieve

real power. By the middle of the thirteenth century, dining halls and dormitories had been added to the lodges, and most had a sitting room and a library for storing architectural drawings. The drawings had become very complex, for the Gothic style had become very complex.

After the lodge, the complexity of the Gothic style was the primary source of the masons' power. Within fifty years of the first Gothic structure, the style demanded a knowledge of engineering and mathematics that monks and bishops did not have time to learn. The masons had learned by teaching one another, and they would not have taught the bishops had they been asked. The masonic lodges had become a network throughout Western Europe; a mason never traveled the dangerous medieval ways with possessions or money of any kind. He would stop at a lodge, identify himself with a secret password and

The German architects who designed Cologne Cathedral (left), the largest in Northern Europe, lacked their French counterparts' sense of proportion. The cathedral's width is insufficiently balanced by its length, and two massive towers all but dwarf the main building. Salisbury Cathedral (above) is characteristic of the English Gothic and boasts that country's tallest spire. The Lichfield spires (right) form the only triple group in England.

exchange of greeting, dine, and make drawings of the latest innovation he had seen. He was given a bed for the night, a fresh horse in the morning, and after examining the building site, he would set out for the next lodge on his route. Through this system the masons were able to keep up with the latest techniques in building and keep their libraries of drawings up to date.

At the beginning of the thirteenth century almost every large town in France and several in southern Germany had cathedrals under construction. The masons were well-organized, well-informed, and eminently aware of their own importance. As a means of flaunting their independence, they favored garish garments of silk and satin and capes with solid-colored exteriors and patterned linings. In his dealings with the bishop the average mason was argumentative and irreverent. But the aspect of the masons' carriage that seemed to offend the bishops most—it was the one that the bishops struck out against, finally—was the length of the masons' hair.

In the Middle Ages, short hair and a clean-shaven face were signs of piety and humility. The masons let their hair grow down to their shoulders and cultivated unruly beards. In the year 1230 the horrified bishops sent out an order: the masons were to cut their hair, and their beards must come off. The masons refused. When the order was restated, the masons refused again and called a strike until the order was rescinded. The Church said there would be no more building in France until the masons' hair and beards were cut. The masons said that they were the ones calling the strike—of course there would be no more building. The bishops threatened imprisonment, trial for heresy, torture. The masons were unmoved. After a standoff of several weeks, the masons issued a proclamation: if the order were not rescinded, the brotherhood of masons would systematically burn to the ground every church, monastery, and cathedral in France. It was an incredible ultimatum to make to the medieval Church, and incredibly the Church rescinded its original demands. Long-haired and bearded, the masons picked up their tools and went back to waging the cathedral crusade.

Masonry was the first profession in medieval Europe to transcend classes. When masons had gone to work in 1100, they had slept in the stables or kitchen with other servants. Only one hundred and fifty years later, they had the same stature as university professors. Furthermore, they still assumed the responsibility for educating future masons. Most of the prospects they selected were youths working at the building trade—poor youths, peasant youths. Masonry provided the opportunity for a peasant to rise to position and real prestige. For after the long-hair strike of 1230, a new relationship gradually developed between bishop and mason—the stimulating, mutually respectful relationship that has prevailed ever since between patron and architect.

Unlike the military Crusades, the cathedral crusade was a success, at least to the extent that it provided virtually every diocese in medieval France and Germany with a fine, individualized Gothic cathedral. In fact, it might be said that the Gothic was the only architecture in history that neither evolved into nor was replaced by a different architecture. It simply did its job, and left it at that.

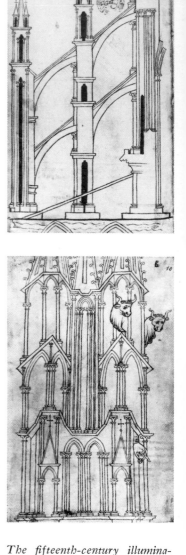

The fifteenth-century illumination at right is supposed to represent the building of the Tower of Babel but more accurately delineates Gothic construction methods. In the rear is the masons' lodge, which provided the craftsmen with a meeting hall in addition to furnishing them with a place to store their tools and the drawings (above) that were so vital to their trade. The top one is a graceful rendering of the flying buttresses that were an essential part of the Gothic style. Beneath it is a whimsical sketch of the tower of Laon Cathedral, complete with representations of the oxen that were carved there in stone.

6

Houses of the Soul

GOTHIC ARCHITECTURE is preeminently religious architecture. The secular influences that were brought to bear on the development of the Gothic notwithstanding, the building of a cathedral was chiefly an expression of faith. It is a truly Christian architecture; it is Christian not merely in function but also in spirit.

And yet the building of a great Gothic cathedral was also a conspicuously human enterprise. It was a virtuoso performance, and the virtuosity of the builders is always apparent—in the technology, in the scale, in the manipulation of space, in the embellishment. Although the edifice may represent a celebration of religious dedication, although God or Christ or the Virgin Mary may be acknowledged as the inspiration for its rise, the celebrant clearly is man. The cathedral is his gift to those he worships; it is his handiwork, and he has taken no pains to conceal his role in its creation.

The Gothic cathedral, then, was more than a monument to Christian spirituality; it was a monument to the Christian men who built it and to the Christian civilization to which the men belonged. This combination of spiritual and social monumentality in religious architecture is the characteristic that, more than any other, brands the Gothic with its peculiarly Western stamp.

It may be argued that the Gothic cathedral took shape according to a set of criteria parallel to the criteria that dictated the shapes of Eastern religious architecture. For instance, in India, the Buddhist stupa—a mound-shaped structure that contained statuary or relics and that was the destination of pilgrimages—was designed to serve the needs of Buddhist ritual. On his arrival the pilgrim was required to circumambulate the stupa; therefore, the stupa was round. As spiritual meditation was an individual and private experience, carried on outside the structure, the stupa was an exterior entity; its division of interior space was relatively unimportant (and in this respect somewhat comparable to Egyptian pyramids). Intended as an object to inspire contemplation and understanding, the form of the stupa was a symbolic representation of the universe; the base was the earth, the hemispheric mound the heavens, and a central mast represented the universal axis. Because the pilgrim was urged, while meditating, to exclude earthly considerations, the stupa was enclosed by a high wall that shut out the sights and sounds of the world.

The Great Stupa, or memorial shrine, at Sanchi is the oldest building in India, dating from the reign of King Asoka—two and a half centuries before Christ—or even earlier. Constructed of solid brick, the Buddhist monument is 106 feet in diameter and 42 feet high and is surrounded by stone railings pierced at the cardinal points of the compass by four ceremonial gateways. Of these, the south gateway (left) is the oldest.

Comparable influences could be said to have dictated the shape of the Gothic cathedral. Inasmuch as Christian prayer at an edifice was a collective experience, presided over by a priest, the cathedral was an interior structure with provision for a congregation of worshipers (the nave) and for an elevated platform (the altar) for the conduct of the Mass. Christians were also encouraged to worship privately, and so small, private chapels were erected in the rounded end (the apse) of the cathedral. And, like the stupa, the overall shape of the Gothic cathedral symbolically represented the kingdom of heaven.

The similarities, however, are superficial. The differences between the forces that shaped Western and Eastern religious architecture were actually enormous; they reflected fundamental differences in the attitudes of Western and Eastern civilizations. A brief comparison reveals how much cultural information is contained in a society's architecture.

The religion of Jesus Christ sprang from the Judaic-Semitic traditions of the Near East, but its great triumph was achieved in the West.

Western civilization was already old when Christianity took hold. Greek philosophy and Roman law, among other less celebrated influences (such as barbarian tribalism), had already shaped the Western mind, and the introduction or imposition of Christianity could not erase patterns of thinking that had practically become genetic. As the Church gained strength and structure, its leaders did not even try to erase these patterns; in fact, they did the opposite. For more than a thousand years—from Augustine to Aquinas and beyond—the most effective Christian theologians were those who successfully blended Christian dogma with the ancient Western philosophical and social tra-

The form of the stupa remained a dominant motif in Eastern religious architecture. As a representation of the cosmos, it attained its apex at Borobudur (below, left) in Java. But it also had its influence on both Hindu and Chinese architecture, as is shown by the eighth-century temples at Bhuvaneshavar (below) in eastern India and at the Pagoda of Sun Yüeh (left), China's oldest such structure, dating from A.D. 525.

ditions. The result was the uniquely Western Christianity that emerged from the Dark Ages and matured in the late Middle Ages.

The Gothic cathedral was the perfect tangible expression of Western Christianity. Like the religion it was invented to serve, it was practical as well as spiritual, materialistic as well as mystical. Nothing points up its Western uniqueness better than the cosmic interpretation of its shape formulated by Saint Bernard and his monastic followers. The interpretation works; the diagrams that show how the Gothic duplicates the structure of the kingdom of heaven are convincing. There is only one problem: the interpretation was fashioned after the fact, after the Gothic had already appeared. It really was less an interpretation than a practical justification for a young, emerging style of religious architecture that everyone seemed to like.

In the Far East—and particularly in non-Moslem India—the approach was reversed. The Hindu and Buddhist monuments of the Orient were, quite literally, religious monuments, their form dictated

by the ritual needs of the religion—and before the fact. The stupas and temples of India and China simply are not monuments to the achievements of man; there are no displays of technological virtuosity; the scale does not relate to the human form. It is true, of course, that the proportions of many Chinese pagodas are models of aesthetic perfection, and that the reliefs carved on the architecture of India are breathtakingly exquisite and magnificently executed. But the beauty of Eastern architecture does not alter the fact that in Eastern religious building, man the maker does not celebrate himself. The Buddhist or Hindu shrine is part of the whole religious process.

Chinese sumptuary architecture was epitomized in the Forbidden City. At left, the main entrance to the city. The central ramp, decorated with dragons, was reserved for the palanquin of the emperor. At right, guests arriving at the Imperial Palace, from a painting of about 1500.

Chinese and Japanese religious architecture changed more slowly than any other architecture in the world; it has had an evolution even more conservative than that of ancient Egypt. Historically, this is fortunate, for, considering how old and highly developed Oriental civilization is, there is very little existing ancient architecture. The reason for the shortage is the material—wood. Wood is a wonderfully efficient material, lightweight, transportable, strong, and workable—but it does not last. Builders in other civilizations learned early to employ more durable substances for their architectural monuments. The fact that the Oriental builder did not do the same does not mean (as nineteenth-century Westerners thought it meant) that his civilization was backward; the Chinese, after all, had metal alloys and paper long before the West, and the existence of the Great Wall proves they knew how to build with stone. Instead it reflects the essential difference in the attitudes that shaped Oriental and Occidental architecture. For in accordance with Buddhist and Hindu (and Jainist and Shinto and Confucian and most of the other Eastern faiths) teaching, the idea of the building is more important than the tangible embodiment of the building—and it is the idea that is permanent.

Materialism is not an intrinsic part of Christian doctrine, but the materialism that has played a greater part in the formation of Western civilization than Eastern has worn its way into the attitudes of Christendom. When the Cathedral of Chartres burned down in 1194, the townspeople were heartbroken. So deep and lasting was the civic depression that the pope had to send a particularly eloquent and inspiring representative to the town to help rouse the populace from its lethargic despair. It is doubtful that the people of a Chinese town would have reacted the same way. They would have either rebuilt a destroyed shrine or not rebuilt it; their decision would have had no effect on the idea of the building. The idea was that the building was

an earthly object and, like everything else on earth, part of a continuing, transcendental process. The structure's wooden frame may rot or burn, but its idea is permanent.

Environmental considerations gave the Japanese a subtly different attitude toward buildings than the Chinese had (but not toward the idea of buildings). Japan is a small, mountainous archipelago subject to earthquakes and extreme weather. For centuries the Japanese have recognized the delicacy of their homeland and have practiced a kind of preventive maintenance—the same constant care and repair that is necessary on a boat. In the winter, for instance, they wrap trees sensitive to cold in a protective covering. This sort of care has been given to important—and not so important—buildings. The most striking example is the Shinto shrine of Ise, located on the southern coast of the central island of Honshu. A wood-frame and thatch structure originally

The examples of Japanese art and architecture on these pages include the pagoda at Horyuji (above, right), the shrine at Ise (above), the Phoenix Hall (left) of the Byodo-in at Uji—south of Kyoto and considered the most beautiful building in the Kyoto region—and (below) a typical Japanese screen.

built in the third century A.D., the sanctuary has, except in times of war, been completely rebuilt every twenty years. Today it looks new, and it is new. Yet it actually has existed in its present form for seventeen centuries. The dimensions and details have remained exactly the same, although changes have been affected—very, very gradually—in the refinement of the embellishment.

Japan has many more surviving monuments than has China. The Horyuji temple complex outside Nara, for example, dates from the seventh century A.D.; its Golden Hall is the oldest wooden structure in the world. The city of Kyoto, one of the world's most important artistic centers, is more than a thousand years old and boasts monuments better preserved than most Western stone monuments from the same era. But it should be repeated that Japan's isolation and environmental pressures —not its fundamental attitude toward buildings—are responsible for the greater number of extant buildings.

The religious architecture of India, Indochina, and Indonesia, where wood was scarce, has been preserved in greater abundance than that of

China and Japan. Perhaps because of its voluptuousness, Indian iconography is better known and better appreciated by most Westerners than the architectural forms on which it appears. Yet those forms are among the most dramatic in all the world's building.

The earliest extant form is the stupa. Begun in the third century B.C., the Great Stupa at Sanchi contains the elements that would characterize non-Moslem Indian architecture for all time; the schematic structure, the symbolic detail, the organic shapes, the early (and earthy) iconography, and a certain indescribable aura that can only be called celestial. Because of these elements, Indian religious architecture appeals to every level of mind and spirit. The monumental stupa at Borobudur, in Java, is a man-made mountain that rises in a series of terraces somewhat reminiscent of the step pyramids of ancient Mesopotamia. Its overall shape and the distribution of detail duplicates the Buddhist notion of cosmological enlightenment. At its base its concerns are worldly; as it ascends it becomes more cerebral, then more spiritual. As the pilgrim climbs its terraces, he is thus exposed to a process of progressive purification. The lowest terraces are square; these are the terrestial levels, their surfaces carved with the sensuous figure-sculpture of India, which captures the sense of earthbound feelings and concerns. The upper terraces, the celestial levels, are circular and contain no reliefs. Rising on these levels are a series of seventy-two small stupas, each perforated so that the pilgrim, as he circumambulates the terraces, can look inside and see the figure of a meditating Buddha. At the very top is the main stupa, undecorated, unperforated, pure.

Overleaf: The culmination of stupa-derived architecture is Angkor Wat, the world's largest religious monument. Apart from its immense scale and beauty of overall design, the Cambodian complex is distinguished by its sculptural ornamentation which depicts scenes from the Ramayana, from Hindu legend, and from the life of Suryavarman II, under whose aegis the monument was completed.

In spirit the Hindu monuments of India and its cultural satellites are similar to the Buddhist shrines, although the difference in ritual requires different forms. The earliest Hindu sanctuaries were caves. As the religion spread, its practitioners followed that precedent, and where no cave was available, they created one in rock cliffs. Finally, when freestanding temples were required, the cavelike quality was duplicated. The Great Temple at Bhuvaneshwar, constructed around A.D. 1000, is a series of man-made rock caves of varied form within a walled precinct. The use of rough-cut rock at this compound is extraordinary; even the word "sculptural" seems somehow inadequate to describe the plasticity of the shapes. There is an almost organic quality to this architecture; it looks more grown than built.

Two centuries after the construction of Bhuvaneshwar, its influence had spread, with the religion that inspired it, to Indochina; and in Cambodia an extraordinary monument was erected at Angkor Wat. Composed of three concentric terraces and nine rock towers—which appear almost to have been dripped into place—the Angkor Wat temple synthesizes a thousand years of Indian religious architecture and iconography. And it symbolizes a world where spiritual achievement was every pious person's goal, but where the realities of the flesh were not regarded with condescension. Today it stands in the middle of a very different world, and it is in constant peril. Fortunately, no conscientious defender of Western-defined freedom has as yet found it necessary to destroy Angkor Wat in order to save it.

Standing both figuratively and literally between East and West is

the architecture of Islam. Islam was more than the embodiment of a religious faith; it was a conscientiously political, expansionist movement launched by the Prophet Mohammed in the seventh century. Largely because Mohammed himself endorsed military conquest as a means to expand, Islam was, at least in terms of the speed with which it spread, the most successful religion-based movement in history. In the Prophet's own time, Islam incorporated almost the whole of the Arabian peninsula. In the century following his death it stretched eastward across Persia into parts of Pakistan and India, extended westward through Egypt and across North Africa, and reached all the way to Spain. Obviously, so large and quickly formed a realm was too divergent to be truly nationalist, but the unity of Islam was achieved much more

Islamic art in general avoids the portrayal of people and animals, but there are exceptions as the rude Byzantine beasts in the Alhambra's Court of the Lions (left) attest. More in the Islamic tradition are the soaring towers and great dome of the mosque and mausoleum of Sultan Hasan in Cairo (below).

quickly than that of Christendom for two reasons. First, Islam was an attractive religion to most of the peoples whom the Islamic armies conquered, and it was tolerant of other religions (as long as practitioners of other religions within the subjected countries acknowledged Moslem rule). And second, Moslem peoples were enjoined not to make war on one another. Therefore, once the spiritual nation of Islam was formed and its subjects converted, Moslem leaders were able to further solidify Islamic unity by encouraging their subjects to fight against the common enemy: Christendom.

Just as Islam was an eclectic society, which absorbed many of the traditions of its divergent peoples, so, too, was its architecture eclectic. However, a certain aesthetic unity was achieved in the buildings throughout the length and breadth of the Islamic world. Here, as in other religious cultures, the ritual demands of the faith dictated the forms of edifices, and those demands were significantly responsible for the formula unity that could make a mosque in Spain somewhat similar to one in India. But Moslem architecture—and all Moslem art—was given further unity by a pair of quasi-religious restrictions attributed to Mohammed himself: one was the restriction against the use of expensive materials; the other was the restriction against imagery. Neither restriction was observed faithfully in every Moslem country—the Pakistani Moslems could not resist the impulse to gild the domes on their mosques, and at the Taj Mahal in India, golden tiles were mixed in with the humbler clay tiles—but both were nevertheless important in the evolution of Islamic architecture.

The Arabs who dominated Islam from the mid-eighth century until the Crusades were the cultural descendants of the Persians, and the Per-

sians had had a long tradition of decorating their architecture with elaborate images. Inasmuch as the Arabs were also the most literal practitioners of Mohammed's teachings, they were not likely to violate the law against imagery—but neither did they want to abandon their affection for decoration. Their solution to their dilemma was to develop a decorative idiom that did not depend on representation of human subjects. In most of their art the solution assumed the form of geometric, floriate, or purely abstract ornamentation—the arabesque. In architecture it took the form of structural variation in order to create decorative patterns with the architecture itself. The arch was oblique instead of round or pointed; domes were egg- or onion-shaped instead of conventionally hemispheric; honeycomb or stalactite patterns embellished colonnades; bright, glazed tiles in an assortment of shapes decorated

The Taj Mahal, built by Shah Jahan as a mausoleum for Mumtaz Mahal, his beloved wife, remains the supreme example of Indian Mogul architecture. Shah Jahan himself is portrayed opposite in a double-paged miniature accepting a gift of pearls (right) from his chief minister, Asaf Khan, as courtiers (left) look on. The enameled cameo, above left, shows him slaying a lion.

walls. As a result, the letter of the law was obeyed but the spirit violated —for Mohammed had intended mosques to be simple, homely edifices, not showplaces or monuments. Then even the letter was ignored. The first mosques had been made of palm trees and clay; the Great Mosque of Mutawakkil, situated in Iraq, is one surviving example that appears to follow the will of the Prophet. But the Taj Mahal, the Alhambra Palace in Spain, and the Mosque of Ahmed I in Constantinople—to name just a few—reveal how far the Moslems departed from architectural humility. When the Byzantine capital fell to Sultan Mohammed II in 1453, the Moslems had no problem converting the lavish and eminently monumental Church of Hagia Sophia into a mosque. They did, however, take pains to remove or cover over the images and replace them with arabesques.

Today Hagia Sophia, a museum, is a symbol of an ideal that has not been achieved. It is a building for peoples of all faiths and all nationalities in a world that could be, but is not, large enough for all the varied peoples in it to live in peace.

7

Princes and Other Patrons

THE FOUNDLING HOSPITAL in Florence, one of the most celebrated buildings in the history of architecture, was famous long before it was finished. Indeed, almost from the day it was commissioned in 1419—two years before the design was published—the structure was a subject of conversation, speculation, and controversy in Florence. While it was under construction its notoriety steadily spread, for Florence was an important commercial center, and visitors from abroad were impressed with the uniqueness of the building and talked about it when they returned home. By the time of its completion in 1445, the hospital—which was not a hospital in the modern sense of the word, but a home for the orphaned and neglected children of the city—had achieved considerable celebrity throughout the Italian peninsula and even north of the Alps.

History has guaranteed the permanence of its celebrity by acknowledging the foundling home as an architectural landmark of extraordinary importance. "Firsts" are as rare in architecture as in any art—most new styles evolve from old, and the line between last-of-the-old and first-of-the-new is generally all but imperceptible. The abbey church at Saint-Denis, the first Gothic building, was one of those rarities; and the Foundling Hospital was yet another—indisputably the first building in the Renaissance style. This distinction notwithstanding, the widespread interest generated by the foundling home at the time of its construction was only partly due to its architectural properties. Of at least as much significance was the implicit political and social character of the historic undertaking.

The patron of the Foundling Hospital was Giovanni de' Medici. In 1419 the Medici were one of several powerful families competing for economic and political domination of Florence. Although Giovanni did not have as many allies as his rivals had, and although his relations with the Church were rather uneven, the head of the Medici managed to hold his own in the struggle. His incredible wealth—he was probably the richest man in Italy—was undoubtedly his chief weapon, but Giovanni also helped his cause by building a large local constituency, which was to a substantial extent a coalition of the poor and the intellectuals.

Long before Giovanni's time Florence had been in the vanguard of a Classical revival in the humanities. By the start of the fifteenth century artists, poets, and scholars were assembling there to engage in a

Bramante modeled his Tempietto (left) on the round temples of ancient Rome. Only fifteen feet in diameter, this architectural gem marks the spot where Saint Peter was martyred.

115

loosely communal search for ancient Greek and Roman manuscripts and artifacts. The antiquities were studied, translated, interpreted, all under the assumption that the Classical arts and letters expressed more reasonable and humane attitudes than did the arts and letters that reflected the Church-dictated, doctrinaire attitudes of the Middle Ages. They were, in other words, using antiquity as a base for formulating a new attitude for a new age; they called the attitude humanism, and the age would be known as the Renaissance, or rebirth.

When he selected an architect for the Foundling Hospital, Giovanni de' Medici went to the intellectual community and sought out Filippo Brunelleschi. A Florentine by birth, Brunelleschi had been trained as a sculptor and goldsmith. In 1401 he had competed with Lorenzo Ghiberti for the commission to design and execute the new bronze doors of the Florence baptistry, and Ghiberti's design had been selected. Thereafter, Brunelleschi turned to architecture, and among the city's intellectual community he was highly respected as a Classical scholar. Early in the century he had searched for, discovered, and studied the writings of the great architectural theorist of ancient Rome, Vitruvius, who, in the first century B.C., had set down the principles of Classical architecture. With Vitruvius' manuscripts in hand, Brunelleschi took far-ranging trips to Roman ruins. He measured, he calculated, he even worked out the mathematical formula for perspective, and he eventually produced a treatise of his own, containing the principles that would become the basis for the Neoclassical architecture of the Renaissance.

The Foundling Hospital, then, served the interests of Giovanni de' Medici in several ways. The fact that it was a foundling home, a refuge for the poor, forgotten, and homeless, served to remind the *ciompi*, the poorest laborers in the city, that the Medici were interested in the comfort and welfare of all people, especially the humblest folk. (Even after

Florence's Foundling Hospital (above) was indisputably the first building in the Renaissance style and the benevolent function it served would seem to proclaim the humanism of the age. But the foundling home turned out to be the exception rather than the rule. More typical of the Renaissance are the fortresslike structures below, the Palazzo Riccardi (left) and the Palazzo Rucellai (right).

they achieved sole power in Florence the Medici continued to cultivate the support of the urban poor; an expression of this was their introduction of history's first progressive income tax.) The choice of architect and the architectural style proved to the intellectual community that the Medici were within the vanguard of the Classical revival. What better way to prove their sincerity, their devotion not only to Neoclassicism but to humanism, than to commission the very first great building in the Neoclassical idiom, and to make the first great building of a great new age not a castle or a church, but an orphanage? And finally there was the message that the Foundling Hospital carried to the Medici's rivals: this magnificent monument was far more than a charity; it was an arrogant assertion in the face of those rivals that the Medici already considered themselves responsible for Florence and therefore masters of it.

Construction of the Foundling Hospital took place early in the quattrocento—the 1400's—a period that witnessed an astounding eruption of creative energy and which more or less officially inaugurated the Italian Renaissance. With the Medici as chief patrons, libraries and academies were established. Such brilliant artists as Fra Filippo Lippi and Masaccio captured the spirit of humanism on their canvases and redirected the whole future of painting, while Brunelleschi's prescription for architecture immediately became architectural convention. Indeed, Brunelleschi's works, along with the buildings of Michelozzi, Alberti, and others, reshaped the face of Florence, and the face they gave the city was a Neoclassical one. As for the power struggle in which the Medici had been involved, it ended in 1434 with the Medici, not surprisingly, supreme.

The Medici dominance, the spirit of humanism, the quattrocento, the physical and cultural flowering of Florence—it was all so vital, so invigorating. And the Foundling Hospital was so splendid a symbol of, so perfect a monument to celebrate the arrival of, a new age of man.

We have mentioned much earlier that the art of building, as a means of communication, usually transmits a different message than the other visual arts. Whereas painting, for example, often reflects the aspirations or values of a society, architecture is more likely to reveal the cultural realities. If this is true, and if we use the paintings of Masaccio and the Foundling Hospital as our vehicles of communication, what can we learn? Masaccio tells us that he, a product of his society, cares about people as individuals, that he is concerned with the pain and suffering and the ultimate uplifting of the human condition. The Foundling Hospital—the very existence of the foundling home, not to mention its status as a great and important work of art—broadcasts the same message. We might consequently assume that for once in history, aspirations and realities were identical—that Renaissance Florence aspired to be a society where human rights and dignity were paramount, and that Renaissance Florence achieved such a society.

We can, of course, assume nothing of the sort, and the trouble lies with the architectural example. We know that the Catholic church was the real power in medieval France because the architectural symbol of the era was the Gothic cathedral that could be seen in virtually every

diocese in the land. But where is the second foundling home? Because it was the first building of a new era, the Foundling Hospital achieved an inordinate amount of attention and was invested with extraordinary symbolic significance. In fact it proved to be an aberration. At least

The Italian Renaissance had its birth in Florence, much idealized in the perspective at right, and that city's founder of Renaissance architecture was Filippo Brunelleschi. His dome for the Florence Cathedral (left) triumphantly blends the new style with an earlier Gothic building. The Renaissance's foremost patrons were the Medici, and the munificence of Lorenzo the Magnificent (below) marked Florence's most glorious era.

insofar as its communicative value is concerned, the Foundling Hospital is painting in architecture's clothing.

Reality in fifteenth-century Florence was more accurately reflected in Alberti's Palazzo Rucellai and Michelozzi's Palazzo Riccardi, almost fortress-like structures arranged around isolated, central open courts. Reality was the small family chapels constructed here and there in the city to make worship a private affair, removed from the community. Reality was the establishment of the patronage system as the moving force behind the construction of buildings. Even in the bleak, antihumanistic Middle Ages, building with a civic function had been to some degree a civic process. But in the age of man, architecture became a matter between patron and architect, pure and simple; great architecture was to be a monument to the two of them. That was the reality.

The patronage system, which for the most part has lasted into the present day, was not really contrary to one aspect of the Renaissance spirit: individualism. For if it was true that Neoclassicism was the basic style of the age, it was also true that the Neoclassical vocabulary was exactly that—a vocabulary—a syntax whose units could be twisted and turned and combined every which way toward the achievement of highly individualized ends. During a four-hundred-year period that began in the Renaissance and ended with—or one might better say blended into—the Industrial Revolution, architecture was truly a fine art. Since a great deal of it was secular, and since just about all of it was paid for by the very rich, architecture itself became a celebration of the material world—and so to a great extent it reflected the values and life-styles of the ruling classes.

However, we cannot assume from this that Europe's buildings for the next four hundred years reflected a decadent architecture; overall very little of it was decadent. The princes, popes, and kings were patrons of the arts, from which they did not exclude architecture. Architects were now full-fledged artists.

And so the architecture of the Renaissance was highly personal, a collaboration between a patron who knew what he wanted and an architect who had certain idiosyncrasies called style; there was not often conflict because the patron chose the architect whose style pleased him. It did not matter what the function of a building was—it could as easily be a church as a palace—the same individualistic imprint marked it as a personal monument rather than a social one. A Gothic cathedral could take a hundred years to build under five bishops and six masons; once its stylistic direction was set it was set, and it evolved to its logical conclusion with a force of its own. Renaissance buildings were not likely to take so long because they were much smaller, more

Brunelleschi's Pazzi Chapel (left) inspired many later Renaissance structures; its barrel vaults and rib-vaulted dome seem almost Byzantine in conception. The most important expression of the Renaissance in Rome is St. Peter's Basilica (above). The work of thirteen successive architects, it owes its superb dome to Michelangelo and its grand colonnade (right) to Bernini.

personal, and the collaboration was the stylistic raison d'être. When a Florentine prince chose Brunelleschi or Alberti as his architect, he was making a statement about his own sophistication, even about his own view of what constituted faithful Neoclassicism. For whereas Brunelleschi's tendencies led him to measure and duplicate every proportion of his Roman models, Alberti's debt to the Romans, less literal in detail, may have been closer in spirit. Brunelleschi put up his perfect Roman copies wherever there was room; but Alberti always designed his proportions and arranged the placement of his buildings with an eye to the site—the street and the neighboring buildings. The differences are quite subtle in their *palazzi*, but are more apparent in a comparison of Brunelleschi's Pazzi Chapel in Florence and Alberti's Church of San Andrea in Mantua. Both buildings are exquisite; Brunelleschi's is one of the gems of architecture. But while San Andrea fits comfortably in its ancient surroundings, striking for its beauty but not for its incongruousness, the Pazzi Chapel reminds one a little of the circular Guggenheim Museum on rectangular Fifth Avenue in New York.

The Renaissance came to Rome just in time to give its architecture to that city's long-needed urban renewal project. The most lavish expenditure in time, money, and talent, was devoted to St. Peter's Basilica and the Vatican, which reflected the personal tastes of all the popes and all the artists who worked on it; not until the seventeenth century,

when Giovanni Lorenzo Bernini adorned the complex with a network of colonnades, fountains, and a foreground piazza, did Vatican City achieve a sense of design unity. The original, early sixteenth-century architect of St. Peter's was Donato Bramante, who had introduced the Classical revival to Rome with his Tempietto, a small, domed circular temple. After the death of Pope Julius II in 1513, Bramante was replaced by a series of architects who kept changing the plans and accomplished very little. But in 1546, the seventy-two-year-old Michelangelo was brought in, and that settled all controversy. Michelangelo restored Bramante's original Greek-cross plan, redesigned the chapels and apses, and strengthened the piers that would support the grand dome that had been commissioned years earlier—a dome unusual because of its elongated, rather than conventionally hemispherical, shape. Michelangelo also designed a portico of free-standing columns of immense height for the exterior of St. Peter's which, if erected, would have been an astonishing sight, but these plans were never carried out.

Michelangelo was also given the commission to design the Capitol at Rome. He produced a fine triumvirate of buildings: the Palace of the Senate, the Conservatory, and the Capitoline Museum. These overlook a piazza, in the center of which stands a statue of Marcus Aurelius.

Once the religious and civic buildings necessary to the restoration of Rome were completed—or well under way—rich Romans went the way of rich Florentines and started building personal churches for themselves, their families, or merely their own glorification. In Rome, unlike Florence, the rich tended to live in villas in the outskirts, so Rome is comparatively free of piazze. But the style of domestic architecture in the Eternal City soon took a peculiar turn: the strict, geometric Classical forms began to loosen up a bit, the forms stayed but how they were used changed; and soon there were shield-shaped roofs, columned, half-turned cornices, and undulating façades, with exteriors and interiors more and more intricately embellished. In France the departure from the Neoclassical was called Baroque; it was not given a name in Italy. San Carlo alle Quattro Fontane in Rome is a good example of what was happening, and so is San Agnese with its elaborate fountain. The Fountain of Trevi would qualify, too, except that it is very late (1732-62), and echoes rather than exemplifies the Italian Baroque.

Bernini was the greatest architect of the Italian Baroque in Rome. As a sculptor, he is famous for the beautiful Fountain of the Four Rivers in the Piazza Navona in Rome. But his greatest work by far was at St. Peter's, where his grand entrance piazza surrounded by 284 columns provides a sense of unity and order where none had existed.

Venice has always had an architectural character of its own, and the

Doge's Palace is a case in point. It was begun in the Middle Ages when the local preference for Byzantine forms was still prevalent. But the builders apparently decided, at some point, that the Gothic style then in vogue in France was not so bad after all, and they added some pointed arches. Nevertheless, for the most part, the palace is Renaissance in character, especially in the decoration of its façades and the court and interior space divisions.

Venice's greatest buildings, however, include structures by one of the most influential architects of any time, Andrea Palladio. Palladio, who was born in Padua and worked in Venice and its surrounding area

during the second half of the sixteenth century, used mostly Classical conventions and only touched on Baroque elements. An ardent scholar, he seems to have picked up where Brunelleschi left off, calculating the proportions and setting down the principles for Classical architecture. But his buildings, particularly his villas, have a flavor never before seen in architecture—a sense of Classical proportion and order combined with warmth and ambiance.

When the Renaissance moved north into France, the Neoclassical and especially the Baroque elements established in architecture were really put to the test. By the late fifteenth century, France had become a consolidated nation with a strong monarch and a large aristocracy. The French were not known for their restraint. The Palace at Fontainebleau was probably the largest residence, regal or otherwise, ever built until the sixteenth century, and perhaps because of its great size the architects did not seem to know what to do with the exterior: it has no unified design, it is something like a street of similar but not identical townhouses. On the other hand, the Palace of the Louvre—begun just eighteen years later—is quite handsome but owes its embellishment chiefly to the Italian example. The real French talent for architectural

The Louvre (right) was begun in the reign of Francis I in 1546 but was not completed until 1875. Its successive stages of construction thus exhibit a complete history of the French Renaissance. The Baroque style was well-suited to the wanton extravagance of Louis XIV. The sums of money spent on his royal residence at Versailles (below) were staggering; the magnificent Hall of Mirrors (left) is but one example of the Sun King's self-indulgence.

Overleaf: Chambord's lofty chimneys and ornate dormers punctuate the Loire landscape.

The stately country chateau at Blois (left) was begun in 1498 and finally completed in 1638. Remarkably, diverse styles from many different periods are blended into a harmonious whole. The imposing Renaissance façade of Les Invalides in Paris (below) is complemented by J. H. Mansart's superb dome, beneath which lie the remains of Napoleon Bonaparte. The excessive ornamentation of Heidelberg Castle (right) characterizes the Renaissance in Germany.

decoration was best expressed in the great country châteaux, such as Blois, where one can see a well-blended combination of styles from a variety of periods—or at the seventeenth-century Château de Maisons near Paris, where one can see the harmony of the French Renaissance style at its best in a building that took just four years to construct. The Baroque entered France on a grand scale at Versailles and became the official architecture of the seventeenth and eighteenth century. In Paris the Church of the Dome, the palaces on the Place de la Concorde, the Hôtels des Monnaies, Lambert, and de Sully are the best known landmarks, after the Place Vendôme. There, as in Italy, the cult of the individual had made its mark on architecture.

Even the Germans gave the Neoclassical Renaissance treatment to some of their buildings, although, as one writer speaking of Heidelberg Castle writes, "Compared with the classical simplicity and restraint of Italian Renaissance achievement, the design of Heidelberg shows a grossness of taste that treats the wall less as building than as a field for decoration." The Gothic was actually very well-suited to the German

national character and climate, and deep down the Germans knew it: the sixteenth-century Stadtweinhaus in Munster, technically a Renaissance building, is imbued with remains of the Gothic; similarly one of Germany's finest structures, the Rathaus Portico in Cologne, combines Renaissance style with Gothic undertones. Oddly enough, where the Renaissance structures had been overstated in Germany, Baroque architecture was comparatively restrained. The Wurzburg Residenz has been compared to Versailles, but almost always unfavorably.

Ultimately, the architecture of the Renaissance and the Baroque became the architecture of self-aggrandizement; it was built by princes, popes, kings, and aristocrats for their own comfort. It was called Neoclassical, it superceded the Gothic, but in fact—though much of it was magnificent—it lacked the human scale and sense of intimacy that had characterized the real Classical; and it lacked the enveloping strength of the Gothic. All it had was grandeur, but all great architecture has grandeur. All other great architecture has something else. It told everybody who was in charge there, when nobody needed reminding.

The architecture of the age of kings, which was introduced by the Foundling Hospital, turned out to be the antithesis of the Foundling Hospital. A follow-up period continuing the spirit of the foundling home did not come right away. So the spirit had to wait. It's still waiting.

We have chosen to deal with English Renaissance architecture separately because the architecture of England has always stood somewhat apart from the architecture of its continental neighbors. The British Isles, after all, stand apart from Europe—not isolated, certainly, not unrelated politically or culturally, but figuratively and literally detached. English history reflects that country's traditional position as simultaneous participant in and observer of the European scene, and so does the development of the arts in England. Moreover, English history, having greater continuity than that of the great nations of the Continent, made the English more cautious about affecting change in their institutions and arts. Sometimes this conservatism has been a positive force, as in Britain's strong literary tradition. In some of the other arts, however, British conservatism has seemed to have had a retarding influence. British painting has had more downs than ups, and though the British have an ancient musical heritage and are among the world's most appreciative music lovers, they have produced no roster of great native composers even remotely comparable to those of the German and Italian states.

On balance, British conservatism has had an effect on architecture that must be counted as positive. If it is true that the building art in England has seldom if ever achieved the passion of German architecture, the lyrical romanticism of French architecture, or the dynamic monumentality of Italian architecture, it is also true that English building has been characterized by a dignity, practicality, and consistency unique in Europe. The English almost never dropped old habits to embrace new styles. When something worked, it was used and reused. And as new styles were introduced to the island, they were phased in, often element by element, and fitted around proven conventions.

The British use of timber provides a good example of how British

Curiously, although Renaissance architecture in Germany was overstated, the Baroque was comparatively restrained. Wurzburg Residenz (right) has little of Heidelberg Castle's excesses. A magnificent Tiepolo fresco adorns the ceiling above the palace's grand stairway.

architecture achieved its remarkable continuity. In the Middle Ages the Gothic came to England, but the builders there did not immediately employ the system of stone vaulting used in the great French and German cathedrals; they retained—though they elaborated on them—their traditional timber roofs. When one considers that the British were shipbuilders long before they were architects this made sense; they knew wood as well as the French knew stone and the Italians knew marble. During the Tudor period—which was the transitional period between the medieval and Renaissance eras—the timber roof was lowered, became more elaborate, and was often left exposed, with horizontal rafters, to become a conspicuously decorative architectural element. On the exteriors of the famous English Tudor mansions, timber was mixed with stone so effectively that the style became a favorite of home builders and inn builders and remains so today.

When the Renaissance architectural forms came to England in the sixteenth century, many medieval elements were retained, and the result was the unique and handsome Elizabethan style, best exemplified, perhaps, by the major colleges of Oxford and Cambridge. Jacobean architecture in the early seventeenth century eased out a few more medieval elements, but not until the Stuart period did something closely approximating true Classicism take hold in England.

Inigo Jones and Christopher Wren were the two great architects of the Stuart period, and together they were responsible for much of London's most elegant architecture. At one time a theatrical costume and set designer, Jones traveled extensively on the Continent early in the seventeenth century and became particularly attracted to the work of Palladio. When he returned to England, he designed a series of exquisite, relatively small townhouses that were so practical, comfortable, and widely admired that a number of other London architects—either voluntarily or in response to demands by patrons—began to design similar homes. Collectively, Jones and his followers and imitators were known as "the Jones group."

Christopher Wren was the British Brunelleschi. Classical scholar and mathematician, he was more inclined than the Jones group toward monumental architecture. His talents and inclination made him the right man for the right time, for when the Great Fire of 1666 devastated London, Wren was the logical choice to supervise the reconstruction.

The Great Fire that ravaged London in 1666 (above) gave Christopher Wren ample opportunity to display his talents. Though he built fifty-two churches in London, St. Paul's Cathedral (below) remains his masterpiece. Its grand dome (right) rivals that of St. Peter's Basilica in Rome.

His most monumental and magnificent work was St. Paul's Cathedral —with its dome rivaling that of St. Peter's Basilica in Rome—but he was also responsible directly or by supervisory influence, for almost all of the sixty-two institutional structures surrounding the cathedral.

Jones and Wren established the tone of British architecture that prevailed until the Eclectic period of the nineteenth century. The European Baroque contributed a bit more fanciful embellishment—as on the homes of the Adam brothers—but the Baroque style did not really take hold in Britain as firmly as it did in Western Europe.

A final word, more than incidental, about British architecture during the age of kings—and all British architecture, for that matter: it is, without doubt, the best-preserved architecture in the world. British buildings last not only because the British people care about their past

and think it essential to preserve the tangible material of the past; they last because British builders care about the future. The condition of their architecture, then, is in a way an endorsement of their conservatism. Be cautious about accepting change, architects seem to have been saying for centuries—not rigid, but cautious; wait until a new way to build is understood before it is adopted. Trust the tried and true. British architecture may not be the most passionate, the most lyrical, the most dynamic. But it is noble, and, more important, it has endured.

8

Looking Back and Looking Forward

THE GREAT POLITICAL REVOLUTIONS of the late 1700's and early 1800's did not trigger a revolution in architecture; instead they inspired still another Classical revival. A revolution of a different sort was brewing in those tumultuous years, however. And though it was far less conspicuous than the upheavals wrought by the Americans and the French, this revolution would have a profound effect on architecture. It was, of course, the Industrial Revolution.

That a revived Classicism should be the first visible architectural product of political revolution is perfectly reasonable. The spirit behind the conflicts that established the United States and rocked Europe was republican, and republicanism and democracy had always been associated, in the Western mind, with ancient Greece and Rome. Moreover, the last Classical revival had also heralded a new age, an age when the dogmatism and brutality of a passing epoch was replaced by the spirit of humanism. When the Renaissance gave way to the age of kings, the spirit of humanism was dissipated, and—one might almost say accordingly—the Classical style was corrupted. A return to Classicism, then, symbolized a return to basics—the basic attitudes reflected in Greek philosophy, Roman law, and Renaissance humanities.

The effect of the Industrial Revolution on architecture was much less direct at first (though in the long run much more profound) than was the effect of the political revolutions. Indeed, even after builders in Europe and the United States learned the techniques of construction with iron, steel, and glass, the effects of the new materials remained inconspicuous; it was almost as if architects were ashamed of themselves for using the materials. They used them, but they covered new frames with façades of old design.

The Classical revival was strongest in the two countries that had made revolutions. In France, under Napoleon, the style was called Empire, and it was not so much a revivalist style as an imitative one. The Madeleine in Paris, for example, which was originally intended as a pantheon and was built by order of Napoleon, is an imitation of a Greek columned temple. It stands on a Roman-style podium that is twenty-three feet high. The Arc de Triomphe, too, might just as well have been built in third-century Rome as nineteenth-century Paris. In the United States a Frenchman, Pierre Charles L'Enfant, designed the federal city of Washington, D.C., as a latter-day, considerably more

The concrete shells of the Sydney Opera House (opposite) billow like sails above the harbor. Although original estimates called for five years and seven million dollars, the structure required sixteen years and more than one hundred million dollars. Meanwhile it caused so many bitter political wrangles that its designer, Joern Utzon, resigned midway through construction and returned to his native Denmark.

Inspired by the Maison Carrée at Nîmes, France (above), Thomas Jefferson designed a state capitol for Virginia that introduced Neoclassicism to the United States. The Hôtel de Salm in Paris was the inspiration for his home, Monticello (left). He also submitted anonymously a sketch for the White House (right), which was rejected in favor of that of Irish-born James Hoban. Hoban built the White House and rebuilt it in 1815, after it was burned by the British in the War of 1812. The engraving (below, right) shows how the White House looked in 1839.

spacious Rome. Interestingly, of all the architects working in the Neo-classical idiom on the two continents, it probably was Thomas Jefferson who was the most inventive.

During his sojourn abroad as minister to France, he fell in love with the Classical style as exemplified by the Maison Carrée at Nîmes—and this was his model for a new state capital at Richmond, Virginia. But Jefferson did not value historical exactitude to the extent that his contemporaries did. He was more like the Renaissance architects who sought to duplicate the spirit more than the letter of Classicism. Monticello, his Virginia home, certainly is Classical in proportion and detail, but it is also remarkably innovative. Jefferson mixed his materials—red brick, marble, and wood—and varied his shapes and volumes to create a building uniquely suited not only to his personal needs, but to the rustic Virginia landscape as well. Classicism and Romanticism in the visual arts are frequently regarded—not unreasonably—as polar idioms, and yet Monticello could fairly be called a Romantic Classical building. It has unexpected nooks and crannies and interior surprises seldom associated with Classical architecture, and another indefinable quality, also rare in the idiom, that can only be called coziness.

As regards Romanticism, this new way of thinking and creating gradually emerged in Western Europe as the tempestuous Napoleonic years ended. In reaction against the rationalism of the Enlightenment,

Romanticism elevated the function of the senses and emotions in the intellectual process. The movement started in England, and in the arts its first practitioners took conspicuous inspiration from medieval art—no surprise, inasmuch as the legends, history, and general aura of the Middle Ages provided a sensual and emotional contrast to the intellectual traditions of antiquity and the Renaissance.

The first expressions of Romanticism in architecture were neo-Gothic. The romantics, however, were not inclined to be literal revivalists; free expression and responsiveness to inspirations from the past in an intuitive way were, after all, significant aspects of the movement. In consequence, architects felt free to select any elements from any architecture, combine them, disregard their relationship to structure, and come up with buildings that appealed to the senses. The formal name for the resulting style was Eclecticism, but more than a few people called the style confusing. "The young architect," wrote the German critic Gottfried Semper in 1834, "travels across the world, stuffs his folder with sketches of every kind, and goes confidently home again in the happy expectation that there soon will be orders for a memorial hall á la Parthenon, a boudoir á la Pompeii, a palace á la Pitti, a Byzantine church or a bazaar in the Turkish style."

Most critics of Eclecticism during its short mid-nineteenth-century flowering disliked it simply because it was impure, but only a man with rare perception realized that the style was odd primarily because its dependency on forms from the past was outdated and inconsistent with the use of new materials. Such a man was the French essayist Théophile

Gautier, who wrote that "when man makes use of the new materials that modern industry can supply, a new architecture will be born." That was written in 1850, when iron, steel, plate glass, and reinforced concrete were available but scarcely being used in building. When they were used, they were more often than not concealed.

But the demands of the times were more compelling than the whims of fashionable architects. By midcentury the Industrial Revolution was in high gear, and to keep it rolling new modes of transportation, new mechanized means of communication, and new types of architectural facilities were needed. What the Industrial Revolution needed, it invariably got; indeed, it provided for its needs itself. Thus the railroad, the telegraph and later the telephone, and finally—a latecomer—modern architecture were at once products of the new, emerging technology and necessary vehicles for the further development of that technology. That architecture would come around in response to the demands of the era was inevitable. It could be said that that inevitability was ensured in 1857. In that year, Elisha Graves Otis installed his first safety passenger elevator in the Haughwout Department Store in New York City, augmenting existing freight elevators.

The Industrial Revolution made the technologically advanced nations of the world into urban-industrial societies. Urbanization had been creeping along in the Western world since the Middle Ages, but medieval urbanization and Renaissance urbanization and urbanization in the age of exploration and discovery had been nothing compared with what was coming. From the very dawning of civilization the principal occupation of people had been the gathering of the necessities of survival; and however much commerce had grown over the centuries, the labor of most workers was still devoted to farming and the acquisition of materials for clothing, shelter, warmth, and defense. Even as the Industrial Revolution ushered in the age of technology, few would have dreamed how extensively mechanized the gathering processes would become in so short a time. And when that happened, the conver-

The basic conservatism of the early nineteenth century was reflected in its architecture. Although many new building materials—and techniques—were available, the Church of La Madeleine (left) in Paris (started in 1806) is a Neoclassical structure, as is the British Museum (below, right) in London (started in 1823). The Houses of Parliament (right), also in London (started in 1840), are noted for their neo-Tudor decorative details and had a great influence on the Gothic revival in England.

sion of materials into goods and the distribution of those goods would occupy the hands that formerly had planted and hunted and chopped down trees.

The manufacture and distribution of goods required centralization. Manufacturers had to get raw materials, arrange financing, acquire machinery, sell their products, arrange for transportation of the goods from factory to depot, from depot to the purchaser. Later they had to have showrooms for their products, advertising agencies to make their products known to the consumer, stock brokers to invest surplus profits. All of these activities became routine parts of the normal week's calendar, and to facilitate the necessary intercourse between manufacturers, suppliers, banks, shippers, advertisers and media, wholesale and retail outlets, and brokers, all would have to be situated within striking distance of one another—in a city.

But if the nineteenth century was a period of enormous growth for American and European cities, it was a period of caution for the art of architecture. The changes that were taking place—the elevation of the importance of the city and the evolution of an architecture that would reshape the city to serve the age of technology—were confusing. The cities, and the architecture, reflected the confusion. London, for many years the heart of the Industrial Revolution, was a case in point. Among the most important building projects in the city dominated by Sir Christopher Wren's eighteenth-century domes and spires were the new Houses of Parliament—a gigantic complex of iron-framed buildings with façades that make them look as though they were built in the Middle Ages. Another important new nineteenth-century structure was the British Museum, and it was given a Classical exterior. Yet the real

character of London in the 1800's was shaped not by architecture but by the influx of people to the city. No one expected such an increase in population in so short a time, and no one dealt with it when it materialized. In his novels, Charles Dickens has left us a clear picture of the character of the city.

New York was virtually a child of the Industrial Revolution; its growth in the second half of the nineteenth century was nothing short of phenomenal. All along lower Broadway buildings with Greek and Roman and sometimes Gothic façades went up to house the courtiers of commerce. Meanwhile shiploads of immigrants arrived day after day, year after year; the real character of the swelling city was symbolized not by the architecture of the business district but by the tenements housing the newcomers.

The nineteenth century was not wholly without architecture that portended the architecture of a new age. For its Great Exhibition at Hyde Park in 1850, London built a massive Crystal Palace, a wide-open glass-and-steel structure that duplicated no past architecture but left its unfamiliar framework exposed. In Paris, Henri Labrouste built the Library of Ste. Geneviève with an exposed iron framework. (The framework was, however, fluted and embellished to resemble Classical decoration, but just the fact that the iron was exposed was an important innovation in 1850, when it was completed.) For the International Exhibition of 1889, the French built the Halles des Machines in the tradition of the London Crystal Palace, and the Eiffel Tower, which certainly made no reference to the past. But except for the library, these examples suggest that really ambitious architecture—architecture that employed the new materials in a stylistic way that was dictated by the nature of the materials—was largely reserved for showpieces, for architecture that was associated with the nonfunctional and slightly bizarre.

Serious architecture had to have at the very least a Corinthian column or a Gothic pointed arch.

That attitude did not begin to fade until the last quarter of the century, and it faded very slowly. It was replaced by the seeds of a functionalist attitude that took different forms in Europe and the United States. In Europe, the changing attitude was first reflected by practitioners of the style called Art Nouveau. This swirling style with its organic-based shapes emphasized the properties of the materials; iron was left looking like iron, even if it was twisted into a vine and leaf design. Art Nouveau produced very few first-rate buildings, but it helped to free the building art from Classical and medieval conventions. Architects who employed it or who watched others employ it were more inclined than before to take liberties with the old conventions and to make more personal statements.

Not every architect went as far as the Spaniard Antoni Gaudí, whose work transcended Art Nouveau and Eclecticism, while drawing on both, and became the architectural equivalent to the Expressionism that was emerging in European painting and sculpture. Gaudí was one of the most individualistic and inspired architects who ever lived. His Church of the Sagrada Familia and Casa Milá, an apartment house in Barcelona, are as personal statements as any work of Expressionist sculp-

ture, so personal, in fact, that they really belong to no architectural movement. Yet Gaudí must be recognized as a uniquely influential architect, even if no one duplicated the idiom in which he worked. For Gaudí's work really freed architecture from the bonds of the past, while recognizing the debt to the past; it seemed to say, "Look back; now move on."

In the United States architecture was transformed through the related works of a great triumvirate: Henry Hobson Richardson, Louis Sullivan, and Frank Lloyd Wright. Richardson and Wright were primarily designers of dwellings; but their use of modern materials to open up interior spaces—to all but eliminate the supporting wall from the inside of a structure, thus making the division of interior space extremely flexible—was influential to all forms of architecture. Richardson, the eldest of the three, was also one of the world's first architects to remove the conventional, revivalist façades from his exteriors. His Marshall Field Wholesale Warehouse in Chicago, completed in 1887 and, unfortunately, demolished in 1930, may have been the most significant architectural landmark of late nineteenth-century America. It was seven stories high—a high-rise for that time—and its exterior of brick was undecorated. Three years later the architectural firm of D. H. Burnham & Co. built the thirteen-story Reliance Building in Chicago; and in the same year Louis Sullivan began the Wainwright Building in St. Louis and the Carson Pirie Scott & Co. store in Chicago. In all three buildings the exteriors were designed to emphasize rather than conceal the basic framework and verticality of the buildings.

The functionalist style pioneered in the United States—and specifically in Chicago by Sullivan and those he influenced—was further refined at the famous German art school, the Bauhaus, during the Weimar Republic. The Bauhaus's two directors, Walter Gropius and then Ludwig Mies van der Rohe, reduced the urban building to a basic

Working primarily with stone and brick, Antoni Gaudí built visionary structures that almost seem to owe more to sculpture than to architecture. Among his creations are the Casa Milá (left) and the Church of the Sagrada Família (opposite), both in Barcelona, Spain. At the same time, on the other side of the Atlantic, Louis Sullivan was working with steel and concrete to help create a new look in urban architecture with such skyscrapers as his Guaranty Building (above) in Buffalo, New York.

framework of steel, a skin of glass, and an open interior in which "curtain walls" could be moved around to suit the purposes of the user.

The turmoil of European politics in the 1930's and then World War II prevented much application of the Bauhaus style in Europe, but it did have some influence on the building boom of the thirties in the United States, particularly in New York City. American architects who were responsible for such structures as the Empire State Building and the Rockefeller Center complex were still wedded to stone, and to the influence of Sullivan, but the simplicity of the Bauhaus idiom, with its stress on exposed framework and absence of added decoration, was certainly evident. (A much more apparent instance of Bauhaus influence in the United States was in Philadelphia, on the Philadelphia Savings Fund Society Building of 1932—probably the first American building in the now familiar glass-and-steel form, although it, too, has some stone facing.)

Frank Lloyd Wright was continuously active while the Bauhaus influence was working its way into American architecture; and he was actually something of a counterinfluence. His Johnson Wax factory complex in Racine, Wisconsin (see page 17), is a rather romantic statement, meandering and carefully landscaped, but every bit as functional as the simpler Bauhaus structures.

Wright believed that architecture was an extension of the environment. The Bauhaus architects never claimed any such thing. But it is interesting to compare the effects of the two ideas, and the reality of their application. Wright was admittedly unfond of cities. His favorite —and best—commissions were homes, usually in the country. His most famous house is probably Falling Water, the Kaufman home that is built right over a waterfall in Bear Run, near Pittsburgh, Pennsylvania. It blends perfectly with its surroundings; yet it is obviously man-made.

The disciples of the fundamental in architecture emerged from the Bauhaus School (above) in Weimar, Germany. Led by Walter Gropius and Ludwig Mies van der Rohe, its proponents advocated a utilitarian starkness summed up in such phrases as "form follows function" and "less is more." A counterinfluence was Frank Lloyd Wright whose more romantic approach is epitomized in his Falling Water, a dwelling built over a waterfall near Pittsburgh, Pennsylvania (right).

It cannot really be said to be an extension of the environment, though, however harmonious the blend. It bears too conspicuously the stamp of its creator.

Mies van der Rohe, on the other hand, never claimed that his architecture was an extension of any environment. His Seagram Building in New York rises up, straight and severe, on an elevated plaza; it is a monolith on a pedestal. And yet on Park Avenue in New York today, what *is* the environment, what does it consist of? Tall, straight, severe, glass-and-steel monoliths on platforms. So completely has the Bauhaus idiom dominated not only skyscraper architecture—which is after all the principal architecture of our time, our own cathedrals—that it has reshaped the city streets and made itself the basis of the physical urban environment. Compare the Seagram Building with Frank Lloyd

Wright's only New York building, the Guggenheim Museum. What is the environment, and which building is an extension of it?

This is not to suggest that Wright was less the genius, or that his dictim about architecture and environment was unsound. It is meant merely to point out that the Bauhaus idiom has been one of the most successful in history, so successful that it has created its own environment. Not only did Mies van der Rohe and Gropius help reshape the American city in the Bauhaus image (both men emigrated to the United States after Hitler closed the Bauhaus); but they directly or indirectly taught a whole generation of American architects to design skyscrapers their way. Philip Johnson; Skidmore, Owings & Merrill; Harrison & Abramovitz; these and a score of other architects and firms, probably the busiest in the United States during the 1950-70 building boom, have made the Bauhaus style their style and the style of the modern city.

There have been others who have not adopted the style just as it arrived from Germany. Such architects as Edward Durell Stone and I. M. Pei have, in very different ways, resisted the coolness—some call it sterility—and structural spareness of the Bauhaus style. Stone has been almost a maverick in his reintroduction of "applied beauty"—façades that provide decorative motifs in contrast to the natural frameworks—to modern architecture. Pei, who prefers reinforced cast concrete modules to steel frames in his skyscrapers, remains closer to the Swiss-born architect Le Corbusier than to Mies and Gropius in his affection for the effects of mass and weightiness. Similarly, Le Corbusier's legacy can be seen in the work of Eero Saarinen, the late Finnish-American architect whose TWA Terminal at New York's John F. Kennedy Airport is like walk-through sculpture and whose granite-sheathed CBS Building broke the period of almost total dominance of glass and steel in New York. Paul Rudolph combines Le Corbusier massiveness with Frank Lloyd Wright spaciousness to create buildings, such as his Yale Art and Architecture School, that invariably create controversy—and simultaneously attract visitors.

One of the best publicized, often written about, and lavishly praised

architectural enterprises of modern times was Habitat, the massive experimental housing complex created for Expo '67, the international exposition held in Montreal in 1967. Designed by Moshe Safdie, an Israeli-born Canadian architect, the complex is comprised of identical modules—huge concrete blocks that stack up one on top of others and form an airy, three-dimensional environment, complete with parks and playgrounds, three levels of streets, and apartments of various shapes.

Habitat was a prototype, and like any prototype it was very expensive to build. However, since everyone realized that the next Habitat would be much cheaper to build, and since architectural writers were all but universal in their praise, there was good reason to believe that this prefabricated complex—its parts manufactured in a plant on the building site itself—would be the first of many Habitats. The day of the mass-produced, high-density urban housing complex seemed to have arrived. One could not help recalling the effect Lever House had when it was completed in New York in 1952. It attracted a great deal of attention—as Habitat had. It was followed by a series of buildings like it—some fine architecture, some poor imitations—but it had set the tone for a whole period of building. Habitat had arrived with similar, if not greater, fanfare. It was assumed that, like Lever House, Habitat would be repeated and imitated. But nothing of the sort happened. Habitat did not launch a period of experimentation and development in urban housing; it remained an aberration.

For the fact of our time, recorded in our architecture, is that people —ordinary people, working people, the populace, the family—are not yet in charge here. Habitats are few and far between; they are freaks, in a way. The great architecture of our time bears the names of the great corporate powers of our age: Johnson's Wax; CBS; Lever Brothers; Connecticut General Life Insurance; the list goes on. There are, of course, important churches: Corbusier's Chapel of Notre-Dame in Ronchamp is probably the most significant religious edifice of the century. There are great institutional structures: the Yale Art and Architecture

Among the modern corporations that have built monuments to themselves are General Motors, whose headquarters (above) in Detroit was designed by Edward Durell Stone; CBS, whose New York City headquarters (above, right) was designed by Eero Saarinen; and TWA, whose terminal building (below) at New York's John F. Kennedy Airport was also designed by Saarinen.

School, the United Nations, the Bauhaus. There are wonderful concert halls and opera houses: the Grosses Schauspielhaus in Berlin, the Municipal Theater in Munster, Buckminster Fuller's Kaiser Aluminum Dome in Honolulu, the Sidney Opera House, the New York State Theater at Lincoln Center. But there is little doubt what the dominant architectural form of modern times is; it is the skyscraper. And there is little doubt who builds the most important examples of the dominant architectural form of modern times: the corporations who need the urban office space to operate in, and who want to build, as every power-that-has-been has always wanted to build, monuments to themselves.

Yet there is a struggle going on, and in a way architecture has been responsible for the urban crisis that has arisen and created the struggle. The struggle is between people who live in cities in an urban-industrial age, who want to save their cities, and who see that for the first time in history, architecture is choking the cities it supposedly serves. In modern times building after building has been constructed—one after another without very much regard for the buildings next to them. Each building is filled from nine until five with people at work, and when the workday ends, they choke the streets and transportation facilities and highways—and leave the city center empty and dangerous. It might even be said that architecture has served the needs of the modern city and suffocated the modern city at the same time. That is not

architecture's fault—architecture never said it should thrive without control, without urban planning; but that is the dilemma it finds itself in today.

Consider it this way: Eero Saarinen's CBS Building is one of the more striking architectural works to be built in New York in the 1960's. It rises grandly yet soberly from a sunken plaza on an avenue otherwise flanked by buildings of shiny glass and steel. The CBS Building is not shiny; it is dark, with dark-tinted windows and dark protruding granite pillars. The best time to look at it is at dusk: the rich, grainy granite still imparts its natural texture and coloring, and the contrast of dark stone and dark glass is just right, more pronounced than in the daytime, but not as sharp as it is at night. As you approach the building, it first appears as a solid, accordion-rippled mass because of the protrusion of the pillars; then, as you move closer, you begin to see the narrow strips of golden light appear through the windows between the pillars; and finally, as you reach the front, you see the whole: the prism-shaped pillars and the rectangular golden windows form a pattern. The changeability of the surface is a nice change from the usual modern skyscraper,

Although most of the important architecture of our times is corporate in nature, there are exceptions. Le Corbusier's Chapel of Notre-Dame du Haut (above) at Ronchamp, France, graphically displays the richness and power of that architect's work and is probably the most striking modern religious structure in the world. Architects have also been producing notable museums, theaters, and concert halls, a striking example being the one in Sydney, Australia (sketch below; see also page 134). But innovative housing projects are largely absent from the list, with the exception in recent years of Moshe Safdie's Habitat (right), erected in Montreal for that city's 1967 international exposition.

Concert Hall

1. Concert Hall
2. Rehearsal/Recording Hall
3. Drama Theatre
4. Drama Theatre Stage
5. Production Rehearsal Room
6. Public Lounge
7. Administrative Offices
8. Administrative Offices
9. Control Room for Rehearsal/ Recording Hall
10. Foyer
11. Exhibition Hall & Chamber Music Hall
12. Car Concourse
13. Restaurant

with its reflecting walls, and it makes the CBS Building a welcome change in New York, a real contribution to the city's shape.

The only way that the CBS Building could have made a greater contribution to the city of New York was not to have been built at all. For that is the dilemma; there is too much architecture, too little space in the modern city. Rarely can a building—even a great building—contribute as much to the city as an empty square block of air. The whole of the city has been forgotten, its tiny parts have been overdeveloped.

We seem to be in for a period of mass projects calculated to not only provide buildings to serve the urban-industrial society, but to make breathing space for the people who live in it. The day of the individual monument may be over in architecture. The day of the planned urban space may be coming. Perhaps it would be more appropriate to say coming back—coming back from the days of the Romans.

ARCHITECTS ON ARCHITECTURE

The United Nations Headquarters (opposite) in New York City was the result of a collaboration among several world-renowned architects, including Le Corbusier and Brazil's Oscar Niemeyer. Responsibility for the final execution of the plans was with the New York firm of Harrison & Abramovitz.

Although he was a complex blend of poet, artist, and engineer, Louis H. Sullivan ultimately adopted the simple maxim "form follows function" as the guiding principle of his work. In The Tall Office Building Artistically Considered, *Sullivan—aptly called the father of modern American architecture—applied the logic of this formula to the design of tall buildings.*

All things in nature have a shape, that is to say, a form, an outward semblance, that tells us what they are, that distinguishes them from ourselves and from each other.

Unfailingly in nature these shapes express the inner life, the native quality, of the animal, tree, bird, fish, that they present to us; they are so characteristic, so recognizable, that we say, simply, it is "natural" it should be so. Yet the moment we peer beneath this surface of things, the moment we look through the tranquil reflection of ourselves and the clouds above us, down into the clear, fluent, unfathomable depth of nature, how startling is the silence of it, how amazing the flow of life, how absorbing the mystery. Unceasingly the essence of things is taking shape in the matter of things, and this unspeakable process we call birth and growth. Awhile the spirit and the matter fade away together, and it is this that we call decadence, death. These two happenings seem jointed and interdependent, blended into one like a bubble and its iridescence, and they seem borne along upon a slowly moving air. This air is wonderful past all understanding.

Yet to the steadfast eye of one standing upon the shore of things, looking chiefly and most lovingly upon that side on which the sun shines and that we feel joyously to be life, the heart is ever gladdened by the beauty, the exquisite spontaneity, with which life seeks and takes on its forms in an accord perfectly responsive to its needs. It seems ever as though the life and the form were absolutely one and inseparable, so adequate is the sense of fulfillment.

Whether it be the sweeping eagle in his flight or the open apple-blossom, the toiling work-horse, the blithe swan, the branching oak, the winding stream at its base, the drifting clouds, over all the coursing sun, form ever follows function, and this is the law. Where function does not change form does not change. The granite rocks, the ever-brooding hills, remain for ages; the lightning lives, comes into shape, and dies in a twinkling.

It is the pervading law of all things organic, and inorganic, of all things physical and metaphysical, of all things human and all things superhuman, of all true manifestations of the head, of the heart, of the soul, that the life is recognizable in its expression, that form ever follows function. This is the law.

Shall we, then, daily violate this law in our art? Are we so decadent, so imbecile, so utterly weak of eyesight, that we cannot perceive this truth so simple, so very simple? Is it indeed a truth so transparent that we see through it but do not see it? Is it really then, a very marvelous

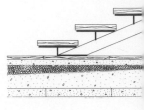

The diagrams above and on the following pages are examples of outstanding twentieth-century works of architecture.

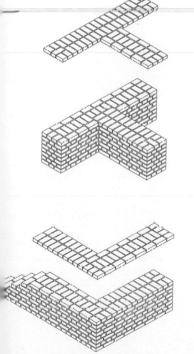

thing, or is it rather so commonplace, so everyday, so near a thing to us, that we cannot perceive that the shape, form, outward expression, design or whatever we may choose, of the tall office building should in the very nature of things follow the functions of the building, and that where the function does not change, the form is not to change?

Does this not readily, clearly, and conclusively show that the lower one or two stories will take on a special character suited to the special needs, that the tiers of typical offices, having the same unchanging function, shall continue in the same unchanging form, and that as to the attic, specific and conclusive as it is in its very nature, its function shall equally be so in force, in significance, in continuity, in conclusiveness of outward expression? From this results, naturally, spontaneously, unwittingly, a three-part division, not from any theory, symbol, or fancied logic.

And thus the design of the tall office building takes its place with all other architectural types made when architecture, as has happened once in many years, was a living art. Witness the Greek temple, the Gothic cathedral, the medieval fortress.

And thus, when native instinct and sensibility shall govern the exercise of our beloved art; when the known law, the respected law, shall be that form ever follows function; when our architects shall cease struggling and prattling handcuffed and vainglorious in the asylum of a foreign school; when it is truly felt, cheerfully accepted, that this law opens up the airy sunshine of green fields, and gives to us a freedom that the very beauty and sumptuousness of the outworking of the law itself as exhibited in nature will deter any sane, any sensitive man from changing into license, when it becomes evident that we are merely speaking a foreign language with a noticeable American accent, whereas each and every architect in the land might, under the benign influence of this law, express in the simplest, most modest, most natural way that which it is in him to say; that he might really and would surely develop his own characteristic individuality, and that the architectural art with him would certainly become a living form of speech, a natural form of utterance, giving surcease to him and adding treasures small and great to the growing art of his land; when we know and feel that Nature is our friend, not our implacable enemy—that an afternoon in the country, an hour by the sea, a full open view of one single day, through dawn, high noon, and twilight, will suggest to us so much that is rhythmical, deep, and eternal in the vast art of architecture, something so deep, so true, that all the narrow formalities, hard-and-fast rules, and strangling bonds of the schools cannot stifle it in us—then it may be proclaimed that we are on the high-road to a natural and satisfying art, an architecture that will soon become a fine art in the true, the best sense of the word, an art that will live because it will be of the people, for the people, and by the people.

LOUIS H. SULLIVAN
The Tall Office Building Artistically Considered, 1896

Frank Lloyd Wright had a remarkably long and fruitful architectural career. One of his earliest notable works—the Winslow House in Chicago—was designed in 1894 while Wright was still on the staff of Adler and Sullivan. For the next sixty years, Wright's work occupied a place in the vanguard of architectural development. Even at the age of eighty-nine he kept busy promoting unique and challenging ideas—including a proposed mile-high office building in Chicago. In two separate books written during the latter part of his career, Wright considered the practical and theoretical components of his artistic outlook.

What is architecture anyway? Is it the vast collection of the various buildings which have been built to please the varying taste of the various lords of mankind? I think not. No, I know that architecture is life; or at least it is life itself taking form and therefore it is the truest record of life as it was lived in the world yesterday, as it is lived today or ever will be lived. So architecture I know to be a Great Spirit. It can never be something which consists of the buildings which have been built by man on earth . . . mostly now rubbish heaps or soon to be. . . . Architecture is that great living creative spirit which from generation to generation, from age to age, proceeds, persists, creates, according to the nature of man, and his circumstances as they change. That is really architecture.

. . . I declare, the time is here for architecture to recognize its own nature, to realize the fact that it is out of life itself for life as it is now lived, a humane and therefore an intensely human thing; it must again become the most human of all the expressions of human nature. Architecture is a necessary interpretation of such human life as we now know if we ourselves are to live with individuality and beauty.

Out of the ground into the light—yes! Not only must the building so proceed, but we cannot have an organic architecture unless we achieve an organic society! We may build some buildings for a few people knowing the significance or value of that sense of the whole which we are learning to call organic, but we cannot have an architecture for a society such as ours now is. We who love architecture and recognize it as the great sense of structure in whatever is—music, painting, sculpture, or life itself—we must somehow act as intermediaries—maybe missionaries.

. . . Let our universities realize and teach that *the law of organic change is the only thing that mankind can know as beneficent or as actual!* We can only know that all things are in process of flowing in some continuous state of becoming. Heraclitus was stoned in the streets of Athens for a fool for making that declaration of independence, I do not remember how many hundreds of years ago.

. . . So modern architecture rejects the major axis and the minor axis of classic architecture. It rejects all grandomania, every building that would stand in military fashion heels together, eyes front, something on the right hand and something on the left hand. Architecture already

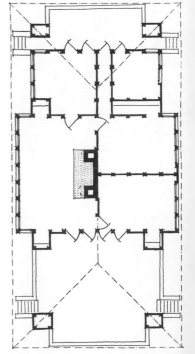

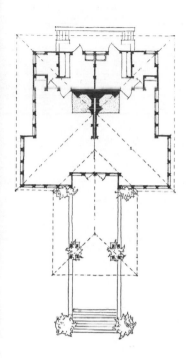

favors the reflex, the natural easy attitude, the occult symmetry of grace and rhythm affirming the ease, grace, and naturalness of natural life. Modern architecture—let us now say *organic* architecture—is a natural architecture—the architecture of nature, for nature.

... Architecture which is really architecture proceeds from the ground and somehow the terrain, the native industrial conditions, the nature of materials and the purpose of the building, must inevitably determine the form and character of any good building.

... No man can build a building for another who does not believe in him, who does not believe in what he believes in, and who has not chosen him because of this faith, knowing what he can do. That is the nature of architect and client as I see it. When a man wants to build a building he seeks an interpreter, does he not? He seeks some man who has the technique to express that thing which he himself desires but cannot do. So, should a man come to me for a building, he would be ready for me. It would be what I could do, that he wanted.

... Architects would do better and well enough were they to stick to their own last and do their own work quietly in their own way. I do not suppose that I myself have much right to be standing here preaching and talking to you of all this except as I have done this thing for a lifetime and swear never to try to tell you of something that I myself have not practiced and so do not really know.

FRANK LLOYD WRIGHT
An Organic Architecture, 1939

As I had gone to and fro between Oak Park and my work with Adler and Sullivan in Chicago, here at hand was the typical American dwelling of the "monogoria" of earlier days standing about on the Chicago prairie. That dwelling got there somehow to become typical. But by any faith in nature, implicit or explicit, it did not belong there. I had seen that in the light of the conception of architecture as natural. And ideas had naturally begun to come as to a more natural house. Each house I built I longed for the chance to build another, and I soon got the chance. I was not the only one sick of hypocrisy and hungry for reality around there, I found.

What was the matter with the kind of house I found on the prairie? Well, now that the "monogoria" of my inexperience has become the clearer vision of experience—let me tell you in more detail.

Just for a beginning let's say, that house *lied* about everything. It had no sense of Unity at all nor any such sense of Space as should belong to a free man among a free people in a free country. It was stuck up however it might be. It was stuck on whatever it happened to be. To take any one of those so-called "homes" away would have improved the landscape and cleared the atmosphere. It was a box, too, that had to be cut full of holes to let in light and air and an especially ugly one to get in and out of, or else it was a clumsy "gabled" chunk of roofed masonry similarly treated. Otherwise, "joinery" reigned supreme. You know—"Carpenter and Joiner" it used to read on the old signs. The floors were the only part of the house left plain and the housewife then covered those with a tangled rug-collection, because otherwise the floors were "bare"—bare, only because one could not very well walk on jig-sawing or turned spindles or plaster-ornament. . . .

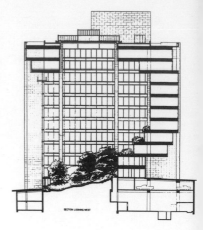

The first feeling therefore had been for a new simplicity. A new sense of simplicity as "organic" had barely begun to take shape in my mind when the Winslow house was planned. But now it began in practice. Organic simplicity might be seen producing significant character in the harmonious order we call nature. All around was beauty in growing things. None were insignificant.

I loved the prairie by instinct as a great simplicity—the trees, the flowers, the sky itself, thrilling by contrast.

I saw that a little of height on the prairie was enough to look like much more—every detail as to height becoming intensely significant, breadths all falling short. Here was a tremendous spaciousness, but all sacrificed needlessly. All "space" was cut up crosswise and cut up lengthwise into the fifty foot "lot"—or would you have twenty-five feet less or twenty-five feet more? Salesmanship cut and parceled it out and sold it with no restrictions. In a great, new, free country there was then, everywhere, a characteristic tendency to "huddle" and in consequence a mean tendency to tip everything in the way of human habitation up edgewise, instead of letting it lie comfortably and naturally flatwise with the ground. Nor has this changed, much, since automobilization made it stupid as an economic measure and criminal as a social habit. I had an idea that the horizontal planes in buildings, those planes parallel to earth, identify themselves with the ground—make the building belong to the ground. I began putting this idea to work. . . .

The first thing to do in building the new house was to get rid of the attic and therefore of the dormer, get rid of the useless "heights" below it. Next, get rid of the unwholesome basement, entirely, yes absolutely —in any house built on the prairie. Instead of lean, brick chimneys, bristling up everywhere to hint at "Judgment" from steep roofs, I could see necessity for one chimney only. A broad generous one, or at most, two, these kept low-down on gently sloping roofs or perhaps flat roofs. The big fireplace in the house below became now a place for a real fire, and justified the great size of this chimney outside. A real fireplace at that time was extraordinary. There were mantels instead. A "mantel" was a marble frame for a few coals. Or it was a piece of wooden furniture with tile stuck in it around a "grate," the whole set slam up against the wall. An insult to comfort. So the *integral* fireplace became an important part of the building itself in the houses I was allowed to build out there on the prairie.

Comforting to see the fire burning deep in the masonry of the house itself.

Taking a human being for my "scale" I brought the whole house down in height to fit a normal one—ergo, 5'8" tall, say. Believing in no other scale than the human being I broadened the mass out all I possibly could, brought it down into spaciousness. It has been said that were I three inches taller (I am 5′8½″ tall) all my houses would have been quite different in proportion. Perhaps.

House walls were now to be started at the ground on a cement or stone water-table that looked like a low platform under the building, and usually was. But the house walls were stopped at the second story window sill level, to let the bedrooms come through above in a continuous window-series under the broad eaves of a gently sloping, overhanging roof. For in this new house the wall as an impediment to outside light and air and beauty was beginning to go. The old wall had been a part of the box in which only a limited number of holes were to be punched. It was still this conception of a wall which was with me when I designed the Winslow house. But after that my conception began to change.

My sense of wall was not a side of a box. It was enclosure to afford protection against storm or heat when this was needed. But it was also increasingly to bring the outside world into the house, and let the inside of the house go outside. In this sense I was working toward the elimination of the wall as a wall to reach the function of a screen, as a means of opening up space, which, as control of building-materials improved, would finally permit the free use of the whole space without affecting the soundness of structure.

The climate being what it was, violent in extremes of heat and cold, damp and dry, dark and bright, I gave broad protecting roof-shelter to the whole, getting back to the original purpose for which the cornice was designed. The underside of the roof-projections was flat and light in color to create a glow of reflected light that made upper rooms not dark, but delightful. The overhangs had double value: shelter and preservation for the walls of the house as well as diffusion of reflected light for the upper story, through the "light screens" that took the place of the walls and were the windows.

And at this time I saw a house primarily as liveable interior space under ample shelter. I liked the sense of "shelter" in the look of the building. I still like it.

Then I went after the popular abuses. Eliminated odds and ends in favor of one material and a single surface as a flat plane from grade to eaves. I treated these flat planes usually as simple enclosing screens or else I again made a plain band around the second story above the window sills turned up over onto the ceiling beneath the eaves. This screen band would be of the same material as the underside of the eaves themselves, or what architects call the "soffitt."

The planes of the building parallel to the ground were all stressed —I like to "stress" them—to grip the whole to Earth. This parallel plane I called, from the beginning,—the plane of the third dimension. The term came naturally enough: really a spiritual interpretation of that dimension.

Sometimes I was able to make the enclosing wall screen below this upper band of the second story—from the second story window sill clear down to the ground, a heavy "wainscot" of fine masonry material resting on the cement or stone "platform" laid on the foundation. I liked the luxury of masonry material, when my clients felt they could afford it.

As a matter of form, too, I liked to see the projecting base or water-table of masonry set out over the foundation walls themselves, as a substantial "visible" preparation for the building. I managed this by setting the studs of the walls to the inside of the foundation walls, instead of to the outside.

All door and window tops were now brought into line with each other with only comfortable head clearage for the average human being. . . .

The house began to associate with the ground and become natural to its prairie site.

Frank Lloyd Wright
An Autobiography, 1932

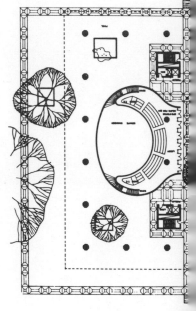

All architects attempt to reconcile two often-contradictory facets of their work—a building's practical function and its artistic statement. In Towards a New Architecture, *a study which served as a manifesto for early twentieth-century architects, Le Corbusier suggested that a resolution of this dilemma lies in the creation of environments more in harmony with people's real experiences and desires than has been the case in the past.*

If we are brought up short by the Parthenon, it is because a chord inside us is struck when we see it; the axis is touched. We do not stop short in front of the Madeleine, which is made up, just like the Parthenon, of steps, columns and pediments (the same primary elements). And the reason is that behind and beyond the grosser sensations, the Madeleine cannot touch our axis; we do not feel the profounder harmonies, and are not rooted to the spot by the recognition of these.

The objects in nature and the results of calculation are clearly and cleanly formed; they are organized without ambiguity. It is because *we see clearly* that we can read, learn and feel their harmony. I repeat: *clear statement* is essential in a work of art.

If the works of nature *live*, and if the creations of calculation *move* and produce activity in us, it is because they are both animated by a unity of the intention which is responsible for them. I repeat: there must be a unity of aim in the work of art.

If the objects of nature and if the creations of calculation gain our attention and awaken our interest, it is because both one and the other have a fundamental attitude which characterizes them. I repeat: a work of art must have its own special character. . . .

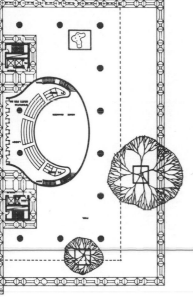

Construction has discovered its methods, methods which in themselves mean a liberation that earlier ages had sought in vain. Everything is possible by calculation and invention, provided that there is at our disposal a sufficiently perfected body of tools, and this does exist. Concrete and steel have entirely transformed the constructional organisation hitherto known, and the exactitude with which these materials can be adapted to calculation and theory every day provides encouraging results, both in the success achieved and in their appearance, which recalls natural phenomena and constantly reproduces experiences realized in nature. If we set ourselves against the past, we can then appreciate the fact that new formulas have been found which only need exploitation to bring about (if we are wise enough to break with routine) a genuine liberation from the constraints we have till now been subjected to. There has been Revolution in methods of construction.

Architecture finds itself confronted with new laws. Construction has undergone innovations so great that the old "styles," which still obsess us, can no longer clothe it; the materials employed evade the attentions of the decorative artist. There is so much novelty in the forms and rhythms furnished by these constructional methods, such novelty in arrangement and in the new industrial programmes, that we can no longer close our minds to the true and profound laws of architecture which are established on mass, rhythm and proportion: the "styles" no longer exist, they are outside our ken; if they still trouble us, it is as parasites. If we set ourselves against the past, we are forced to the conclusion that the old architectural code, with its mass of rules and regulations evolved during four thousand years, is no longer of any interest; it no longer concerns us: all the values have been revised; there has been revolution in the conception of what Architecture is.

Disturbed by the reactions which play upon him from every quarter, the man of to-day is conscious, on the one hand, of a new world which is forming itself regularly, logically and clearly, which produces in a straightforward way things which are useful and usable, and on the other hand he finds himself, to his surprise, living in an old and hostile environment. This framework is his lodging; his town, his street, his house or his flat rise up against him useless, hinder him from following the same path in his leisure that he pursues in his work, hinder him from following in his leisure the organic development of his existence, which is to create a family and to live, like every animal on this earth and like all men of all ages, an organized family life. In this way society is helping forward the destruction of the family, while she sees with terror that this will be her ruin.

There reigns a great disagreement between the modern state of mind, which is an admonition to us, and the stifling accumulation of age-long detritus.

The problem is one of adaptation, in which the realities of our life are in question.

Society is filled with a violent desire for something which it may obtain or may not. Everything lies in that: everything depends on the effort made and the attention paid to these alarming symptoms.

Architecture or Revolution.

Revolution can be avoided.

LE CORBUSIER
Towards a New Architecture, 1927

The gap between dream and reality in housing construction is just as great today as it was in 1938 when R. Buckminster Fuller, the maverick engineer and social planner, satirized the chaotic and wasteful procedures usually followed when building a house.

If, today a man, wishing to acquire an automobile, were to visit one of five thousand automobile designers in New York City, equivalent to New York's five thousand architects, and were to commence his retention of the designer by the limitation that he wanted the automobile to resemble outwardly a Venetian gondola, a jinricksha of the Tang Dynasty, a French fiacre, or a Coronation Coach of Great Britain, pictures of which he had obligingly brought with him, all final embellishment, of course, to be left to the election of his wife; and he and the "designer" were together to pick and choose (from automobile accessory catalogues, advertisements, and "shows") motors, fly wheels, fenders, frame parts offered in concrete, brass, sugar cane fibre, walnut, *et cetera*, and succeeded in designing an automobile somewhat after the style of some other fellow; and they were then to have the design bid upon by five local garages in Queens Village, picking one of the bidders for his ability, or price; and the successful bidder, chosen, let us say, because of his having built grandfather's velocipede, were to insist on the use of some other wheels than those specified; and the local bank, in loaning the money to the prospective "owner" to help him finance, had some practical man look over the plans so that, guessing at the cost, he might base a loan thereon, incidentally insisting on the replacement of several parts and methods by others in which the bank was "interested"; and then the insurance company were to condemn a number of the units used because they had not been paid for their "official approval" and compel the substitution of other units; and fifty material and accessory manufacturers' salesmen were informed by a reporting agency, whose business it was to ferret out this poor man's private plans, that he was going to "build" a car, and were to begin hounding him with specious promises; and, finally, if the local town council had to approve of the design and materials and give a permit for the automobile's construction, sending around assertive inspectors, while it was being erected, it is certain that few of those desiring automobiles would have the temerity to go through with the ardors of acquiring them on such a "craft" and "graft" basis. Should they have the hardihood, the automobile would finally cost in the neighborhood

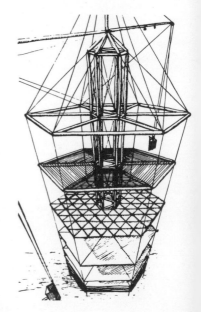

of $50,000, and be highly unsatisfactory, being full of "bugs," and completely without service when finished.

This is exactly the condition in the home building field. Is it any wonder people crowd the city apartment? In the building of such an automobile, not one but many ill trained mechanics from different oddly named "trades" would have to be employed, "carpenters" to apply the carburetor and "masons" to assemble the chassis frame, though many times there would be but room for one man to work. The contractor, who would also be building other cars in Far Rockaway, Roslyn, *et cetera*, would stop in for an hour a day to look over the work, outside of which the job would receive no organization of method. There would probably be strikes by the plumbers or electricians who would insist on most of the improvements in design being left out due to their having no "jurisdiction" permitting them. To cap all, the car would take from six months to a year to build, inasmuch as mechanics in the building trades average 30 steps per net useful contact today as opposed to ½ step in highly developed modern factory conditions, which fact, coupled with the consideration of high discomfiture of building trades' exposed working conditions, and the fact that it is bound by insurance companies to be second only to coal mining in point of fatal accident, indicates the extraordinary change of status that will occur in new housing industry, when mechanics will perform effective shelter service, economically rewarding such labor on an efficacy basis, indicative of wages many times higher than the present scale.

It is a law of evolution and design that designs, whether by man or by "nature," are reproduced in direct proportion to their mechanical adequacy of satisfaction of universal requirements, whether it be a book, a rose, a pencil or a baby. . . .

. . . the development of public enlightenment and industrial management awareness is bringing with it recognition of the fact that any economic survival plan for industry must include not only accredited primary survival of shelter, but the expansion of shelter design to the point of maximum efficiency. Shelter of the human life process involves, in its most comprehensive meaning, consideration of all forces acting to retard or destroy it. It represents the measure of man's intuitive and conscious mastery of equilibrium.

A new dwelling service industry must inevitably develop, even to the point of commanding all other industries.

HOUSES, like other instruments, have not only to be SCIENTIFICALLY DESIGNED but MUST BE PRODUCED, otherwise designers are going to be justly condemned for bringing about academic esthetic race suicide through a battle of words. . . .

Obviously, with the achievement of adequate housing, existing theories of land economics must undergo a profound change, and as the new dwelling service industry correlates and engulfs other industries architecture itself will become enlarged in scope and definition.

The function of the architect will be to RAISE the level of universal existence to the progressively HIGHEST standard of survival and growth. This will manifest the EVOLUTIONARY COURSE of human growth as opposed to the revolutionary, lazy, stop-short method of levelling high standards of existence down to the lowest common denominator to satisfy an inferiority complex and excuse the political imposition of a devastating "class" wedge upon the masses.

The function of the architect-engineer will be the irrevocable integration into society of an universally accredited primary survival. This will be done through the adequate disposition of a constantly improving, available "best" shelter, clothing and sustenance, in a world which can already—through the effort of one man out of every five working but one day a month—produce and distribute the goods and services necessary to all.

Resourcefulness and industriousness, in the conscientious perusal of the myriad of available technological data for the integration involved, will triumph. Buck-passing of technical responsibility and hopeful guessing, progressively self-invalidating, will cease to be profitable.

The proper activity of the architect-engineer is purposeful. "It is not to devise a better society so as to arrive at a finer architecture; it is to provide a better architecture in order to arrive at a more desirable society." [Theodore Larson] The combined function of architect, industrialist and synchronizing architect-engineer, since WHAT to do is known, is, first to determine not causes but purposes, and, then, acting within this knowledge, to evolve an adequate shelter design that will make possible the rational and spiritual self-realization toward which man has ever so longingly striven.

R. BUCKMINSTER FULLER
Nine Chains to the Moon, 1938

The Finnish-born architect Eero Saarinen is responsible for some of the most critically acclaimed structures built since the end of World War II. The Gateway Arch in St. Louis, the Trans World Airlines Building at New York's John F. Kennedy International Airport, the Dulles International Airport in Chantilly, Virginia, and the CBS Building in New York City are milestones in a career tragically cut short by Saarinen's death at age fifty in 1961. In little more than a decade of intense work Saarinen realized many of the principles he gracefully outlined in a speech delivered to students of Dickinson College.

I think of architecture as the total of man's man-made physical surroundings. The only thing I leave out is nature. You might say it is man-made nature. It is the total of everything we have around us, starting from the largest city plan, including the streets we drive on and its telephone poles and signs, down to the building and house we work and live in and does not end until we consider the chair we sit in and the ash tray we dump our pipe in. It is true that the architect practices on only a narrow segment of this wide keyboard, but that is just a matter of historical accident. The total scope is much wider than what he has staked his claim on. So, to the question, what is the scope of architecture? I would answer: It is man's total physical surroundings, outdoors and indoors.

Now, what is the purpose of architecture? Here again I would stake out the most ambitious claim. I think architecture is much more than its utilitarian meaning—to provide shelter for man's activities on earth. It is certainly that, but I believe it has a much more fundamental role to play for man, almost a religious one. Man is on earth for a very short time and he is not quite sure what his purpose is. Religion gives him his primary purpose. The permanence and beauty and meaningfulness of his surroundings give him confidence and a sense of continuity. So, to the question, what is the purpose of architecture, I would answer: To shelter and enhance man's life on earth and to fulfill his belief in the nobility of his existence. . . .

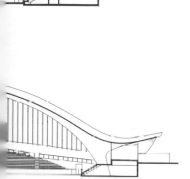

I am a child of my period. I am enthusiastic about the three common principles of modern architecture: function, structure, and being part of our time. The principle of respecting function is deeply imbedded in me as it is in others of this period. But, like others, I do not look to it to solve my architectural problems. Sometimes, however, the problem and the time are ripe for an entirely new functional approach to a problem (as in the new jet airport for Washington), and at such moments function may become the overwhelming principle in directing the formula of design.

The principle of structure has moved in a curious way over this century from being "structural honesty" to "expression of structure" and finally to "structural expressionism." Structural integrity is a potent and lasting principle and I would never want to get far away from it. To express structure, however, is not an end in itself. It is only when structure can contribute to the total and to the other principles that it is important.

The third common principle of modern architecture—the awareness of the thinking and technology of our time—is for me an ever-present challenge. I want always to search out the new possibilities in new materials of our time and to give them their proper place in architectural design.

Yes, I am dedicated to these three basic principles of modern architecture. But it seems to me they are not necessarily the only pillars one's work must rest on. The great architecture of the past did not rest on these alone. There are other principles equally or more important.

When I approach an architectural problem, I try to think out the real significance of the problem. What is its essence and how can the total structure capture that essence? How can the whole building convey emotionally the purpose and meaning of the building? Convey-ing significant meaning is part of the inspirational purpose of architecture and, therefore, for me, it is a fundamental principle of our art.

The conviction that a building cannot be placed on a site, but that a building grows from its site, is another principle in which I believe. I see architecture not as the building alone, but the building in relation to its surroundings, whether nature or man-made surroundings. I believe very strongly that the single building must be carefully related to the whole in the outdoor space it creates. In its mass and scale and material it must become an enhancing element in the total environment. Now this does not mean that the building has to succumb to the total. Any architecture must hold its head high. But a way must be found for uniting the whole, because the total environment is more important than the single building.

The external form of my work varies greatly. But inside the solution of every problem there are underlying principles that hold it together and join each building I have done to every other one. In fact, if it didn't sound too pompous, I would say that the common denominator of my work is the constant philosophy—the constant respect for the principles in which I believe.

Eero Saarinen
Remarks at Dickinson College, 1959

The opening of Lever House on Park Avenue in New York City ushered in a new era in the design and construction of office buildings. A team of architects from the firm of Skidmore, Owings & Merrill worked on the project under the direction of Nathaniel Owings, who found himself fulfilling a dream as well as revolutionizing his profession.

Lever House was built in 1952 but goes back to 1946 in Chicago, where, in a gesture of frustration, I expressed my last full measure of despair at the positively Stone Age attitude of all the office building managers of the world, individually and collectively. I felt that they were to the building industry what railroad unions (who require firemen on diesel engines) were to the railroads. I was tired of remodeling ancient though beautiful relics of a bygone but lucrative age. This tight little group who stood in the way of rebuilding the central city should be stung into some action—or reaction—and I arranged a debate with their acknowledged prophet, George Bailey, on "The Office Building of the Future"; or, as he put it, "The Building That Will Never Be Built." This was staged at the 1949 National Convention of Office Building Owners and Managers at Hot Springs, Virginia, said location guaranteeing a full audience on this, to me, important occasion. By way of a scarehead I sketched the bleak and grimy visage of Wall Street, La Salle Street and Montgomery Street, deserted and empty while the suburbs flourished. As an alternative to this I suggested action smack in the center of the downtown business districts anywhere in America. No less than half a city block would do. There, in the setting

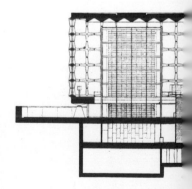

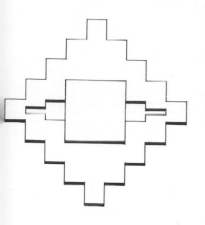

of a park with a garage under it to pay for the land—which was the equivalent of suggesting the transplanting of Walden Pond to La Salle Street—a slender shaft would rise on only a small part of the whole. The shaft would be sealed, free from dirt and sound. . . .

The idea fell flat and lay moribund until George Fry and I got drunk together on New Year's Eve two years later. A consultant to businessmen on how to run their affairs, he often explained that he was willing to put his own problems aside in order to solve theirs. We usually spent New Year's Eve together. This time we got involved in a crap game, and after a long run on the dice I seemed to have all George's money. At this point I felt so sorry for him that I gave it all back and he in turn was so moved that he asked me to help in a confidential matter of business. The business involved Lever Brothers in Boston, and within two weeks I had the contract for their new building, location yet to be determined.

I remember meeting the then president, Charles Luckman, who was a good client, and any unkind suggestions that he picked their particular site on Park Avenue for Lever House so he could watch the building being built from his apartment at the Waldorf are apocryphal.

But there was a time during the early part of the design period when some thought he went a little too far. The topmost floor of the building—the twenty-first floor, the size of a modest house site in the suburbs—had been laid out by Luckman for the personal requirements of the chief executive of the company, Mr. Luckman himself. It contained an exercise room, luxury apartment, dining room and board room and, almost as an afterthought, tucked away was an office. Along the south side of the building a long balcony projected where Luckman could survey the city at his leisure. One day while he was studying the model of the building in our office, he questioned the height of the railing on the balcony. "Three feet," we said. "Why, Charlie, are you afraid you'll fall?" "No, be pushed," he said.

Lever House turned out to be news. An empty lot wasn't news, but as soon as we cleared the taxpayers from the one on Park Avenue between Fifty-third and Fifty-fourth, planted it with trees, shrubs and flowers, and then put a building over it starting at the second floor in such a way that the park remained—that was news.

When we put the narrow tower, just wide enough for two sets of offices and a corridor between, with its narrow end toward the avenue —that was news. All other towers were broadside to the avenue up until then.

When we put parking underneath the park, and another park on top of the pavilion, too—that was news.

Lever House was completed in April of 1952 and was immediately hailed as "handsome, inventive, remarkable." Twenty-one-story Lever House on New York's Park Avenue filled the block between Fifty-third and Fifty-fourth streets and was designed to house 1250 employees. It was air-conditioned (new then) and fluorescent-lit, and every inch of the 290,000 square feet of office space within 25 feet of the windows. The building cost six million dollars (about eighteen million today), and we could "kick away" two hundred and fifty thousand dollars a year in ground-floor rentals in order to leave room for a patio to create the illusion of no ground floor. Critics called the structure "dazzling" and suggested that it had been conceived in part as an advertisement for the company, ranking along with the Empire State Building as a "monument to American industry"—although the critics were quick to point out that the owners were Dutch and English.

We could answer queries from the press with: "We were fortunate in having clients who were aware of advertising and prestige. They didn't want just any building, they wanted Lever House. They let us get away from the tired shape of the ziggurat form of the standard New York office building." . . .

I consider that I contributed two basic ideas to the design: first, the nonbuilding or park at street level; second, the placement of the tower perpendicular to the avenue instead of parallel. Beyond this, all the credit goes to Gordon Bunshaft, designer in charge.

People were impressed that we hadn't hung a big sign on the building saying "Lever House," and the building became better known than if we had. Lever became an important word. Even taxi drivers talked about it and told stories of how sailors sometimes bribed them to drive their cabs over the curb onto the plaza and wind their way in and out between the pillars; of one nice couple who had pulled in under cover on a rainy Sunday to fix a tire; and how children roller-skated on the paths in the little garden.

We thought we knew something about glass. We had researched everything from glass balls spun into fiber (we had helped invent a machine to do that) to huge panes of plate glass in colors to separate out certain rays and cut down heat. We decided to seal the clear, straight shaft with sheets of tinted glass. The wall around our shaft would rise from the street level to the twenty-first floor, a sheer unbroken exterior surface of three hundred and thirty-nine feet; and, except where floor spandrels occurred, just one quarter of an inch thick.

In 1950 Park Avenue was still lined with beautiful, nearly authentic Renaissance palaces. The luxurious Marquery Apartment House was typical. Designed by John Russell Pope, it faced on tree-lined courts, giving the avenue a quiet elegance which was further enriched by Saint Bartholomew's Church, designed by Bertram Grosvenor Goodhue; and McKim, Mead and White's masterpiece, the Racquet Club. Then there was that very special vacant lot: the block between Fifty-third and Fifty-fourth streets. In 1952 Lever House was built there and added its own slender beauty to the lovely old-world charm of that part of Park Avenue.

Then shortly sad things began to happen to the avenue, things we had not anticipated. It appeared that the wide publicity Lever House received gave other corporate giants the idea of seeking the advertising value of this beautiful design, Seagram's for one. Then followed a series of progressively aggressive structures, causing the demolition one by one of the richly clad residential landmarks until only the Racquet Club remained.

One might ask why Lever House caused such a stir, and is still looked upon as an important prototype of modern architecture in a city where skyscrapers are a dime a dozen and where Lever-size buildings are torn down to make room for skyscrapers. Lever House is only a yard taller than the 1903 Flatiron Building. It is smaller than the smallest of the Rockefeller Center buildings, on a lot less than one-twelfth the land on which the Center sits. Its highest main structure is only two stories high and only fifty feet of it touch the valuable Park Avenue frontage, while the Lever tower itself is perpendicular to it. Why does this combination create such a stir? Is it possible for us to fully comprehend the technical triumph of a building·sheathed by a sheet of glass a quarter of an inch in thickness?

When one can predict with certainty which play on Broadway will be a hit, then this question of what constitutes great art in building can also be answered. There are so many separate factors, each with a distinct influence on the ensemble, none under any individual control, that such predictions become impossible. Unlike painting, sculpture or even musical composition, design is the product of the sum total of often unpredictable events. The creation of that product is not done by the architect alone but by all the other elements as well. If the outcome is successful, that is a miracle.

NATHANIEL ALEXANDER OWINGS
The Spaces In Between, 1973

With more than fifty years of architectural achievement behind him, Walter Gropius at seventy-eight possessed a clear perspective on current fads and fashions engulfing his profession. Instead of seeking one answer to the question of how to create a livable environment, Gropius suggested a new approach—"unity in diversity."

The architect is in an ambiguous position in his relation to society and in his double role as a citizen and a professional. Armed to the teeth with technical intricacies, design theories, and philosophical arguments, he still so rarely succeeds in pulling his weight in the public domain where decisions are made which vitally affect his interests. Since popular opinion holds him responsible for the condition of our cities, towns, and countryside, I would like to examine where he stands in this respect and which avenues of action are open to him to broaden his influence.

There are now certain "rumbles" in the architectural profession which have interested me as much as they have baffled me. Since architects possess in general a sensitive, built-in thermometer which registers the crises and doubts, enthusiasms and fancies of their contemporaries, we should listen to the notes of misgiving and warning emerging from their ranks.

All reports made lately by architects and educators on the state of architecture in the sixties are dominated by two words: confusion and chaos. It seems to them that the inherent tendencies of an architecture of the twentieth century, born fifty years or so ago and, then, a deeply felt, indivisible entity, have been exploded into so many fractions that it becomes difficult to draw them together to coherence again. Technical innovations, first greeted as delightful new means to an end, are seized separately and set against each other as ends in themselves; personal methods of approach are hardened into hostile dogmas; a new awareness of our relationship to the past is distorted into a revivalist spirit; our financial affluence is mistaken for a free ticket into social irresponsibility and art-for-art's-sake mentality; and our young people feel bewildered rather than inspired by the wealth of means at their disposal. They are either trying to head for safe corners with limited objectives, or are succumbing to a frivolous application of changing patterns of styling in architecture. In short, we are supposed to have lost direction, confidence, and reverence. Everything goes. . . .

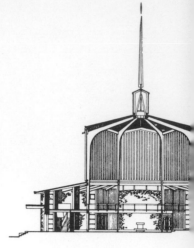

Having been in the crosscurrents of architectural development for over half a century, I find that an architect who wants to help mould the evolutionary forces of his time, instead of letting himself be overcome by them, must distinguish between two sets of components which are apt to influence and direct his work. The first one consists of the human trends which gradually move a society towards new patterns of living; the second consists of the contemporary technical means and individual choices of expression which help these trends to take shape. It is imperative never to lose sight of the first while embroiled with the second, because the architect is thus in danger of losing himself in the design by way of technical stunts or personal mannerisms.

The potentialities of the new technical means fascinated my generation just as much as they do the architect of today, but at the beginning of our movement stood an idea, not an obsession with specific forms and techniques. The activities of life itself were under scrutiny. How to dwell; how to work, move, relax; how to create a life-giving environment for our changed society: this was what occupied our minds. Of course we went about the task of realizing such aims in very different ways, but I do not see why this diversity should by itself cause confusion, except to those who naively believe that there is always only one perfect answer to a problem. There are, of course, many technical and formal approaches to the same task, and any one of them may be successful, if it is well suited to the purpose of the building and to the temperament of the architect; if it is used with discrimination in its given environment. . . .

The common characteristics which clearly emerged from all these innovations are: an increase in flexibility and mobility; a new indoor-outdoor relationship; and a bolder and lighter, less earthbound architectural appearance. . . .

Considering the reservoir of rich talent and the wealth of technical and financial resources available today, it would seem that this generation holds all the aces in the age-old game of creating architectural forms for the ideas by which society lives. Only a magic catalyst seems to be needed to combine these forces and free them from isolation. I personally see this catalyst in the power of education; education to raise the expectations and demands a people make on their own form of living; education to waken . . . latent capacities for creation. . . .

Creativity of the makers needs the response of all the users. I am convinced that a surprising amount of individual whimsey—yes, even aberration and downright ugliness—could be tolerated without causing serious harm, if only the grand design, the image a society should have of itself, would emerge clearly and unequivocally. What we admire in the achievements of city builders of the past is the fact that their work reveals so clearly the ultimate destination of each individual feature as an organic part of the whole. This was what made the city perform its functions well and gave the people a stimulating background for all their activities. How else can the marvel of the Piazza San Marco, this arch-example of perfection, be explained? Not the work of a single master . . . we find instead that . . . a perfect balance was developed between the contributions of a number of architects, using many different materials and methods. They achieved this miracle because they never violated the main purpose of the general plan, yet never forced uniformity of design. San Marco is an ideal illustration of my credo "unity in diversity," to the development of which . . . I can only hope to have made my personal contribution during a long life of search and discovery.

WALTER GROPIUS
Address at Columbia University, 1961

The late Louis I. Kahn is famous for his unconventional approach to architectural design as evidenced in such diverse buildings as the Kimball Museum of Art in Fort Worth, Texas, the Richards Medical Research Building at the University of Pennsylvania, and the Yale University Art Gallery. Kahn displayed the same iconoclastic attitudes in his writings, as can be seen in the following discussion of the importance of form and design in architecture.

All that we desire to create has its beginning in feeling alone. This is true for the scientist. It is true for the artist. . . .

When personal feeling transcends into Religion (not a religion but the essence religion) and Thought leads to Philosophy, the mind opens to realizations. Realization of what may be the *existence will* of, let us say, particular architectural spaces. Realization is the merging of

171

Thought and Feeling at the closest rapport of the mind with the Psyche, the source of *what a thing wants to be*.

It is the beginning of Form. Form encompasses a harmony of systems, a sense of Order and that which characterizes one existence from another. Form has no shape or dimension. For example, in the differentiation of a spoon from spoon, spoon characterizes a form having two inseparable parts, the handle and the bowl. A spoon implies a specific design made of silver or wood, big or little, shallow or deep. Form is "what." Design is "how." Form is impersonal. Design belongs to the designer. Design is a circumstantial act, how much money there is available, the site, the client, the extent of knowledge. Form has nothing to do with circumstantial conditions. In architecture, it characterizes a harmony of spaces good for a certain activity of man. . . .

Giotto was a great painter because he painted the skies black for the daytime and he painted birds that couldn't fly and dogs that couldn't run and he made men bigger than doorways because he was a painter. A painter has this prerogative. He doesn't have to answer to the problems of gravity, nor to the images as we know them in real life. As a painter he expresses a reaction to nature and he teaches us through his eyes and his reactions to the nature of man. A sculptor is one who modifies space with the objects expressive again of his reactions to nature. He does not create space. . . . An architect creates space.

Architecture has limits.

When we touch the invisible walls of its limits then we know more about what is contained in them. A painter can paint square wheels on a cannon to express the futility of war. A sculptor can carve the same square wheels. But an architect must use round wheels. Though painting and sculpture play a beautiful role in the realm of architecture as architecture plays a beautiful role in the realms of painting and sculpture, one does not have the same discipline as the other. . . .

An architect from India gave an excellent talk at the University about the fine new work of Le Corbusier and about his own work. It impressed me, however, that these beautiful works he showed were still out of context and had no position. After his lecture I was asked to remark. Somehow I was moved to go to the blackboard where I drew in the centre of the board a towering water tower, wide on top and narrow below. Like the rays of a star, I drew aqueducts radiating from the tower. This implied the coming of the trees and fertile land and a beginning of living. The buildings not yet there which would cluster around the aqueduct would have meaningful position and character.

The city would have form, expressing its nature.

From all I have said I do not mean to imply a system of thought and work leading to realization from Form to Design.

Designs could just as well lead to realizations in Form.

This interplay is the constant excitement of Architecture.

Louis I. Kahn
Lecture, 1960

172

The strength and clarity visible in Ludwig Mies van der Rohe's most famous structure, the Seagram Building on New York's Park Avenue, represent the distillation of more than fifty years of architectural experience and the application of principles that have formed the foundation of modern architecture. For the most part, Mies refrained from writing or talking about his work. But he did make a short address at dedication ceremonies for the new Chicago campus of the Illinois Institute of Technology—for which he created the master plan and several buildings—and took that opportunity to consider eloquently the dilemma and challenge of twentieth-century architecture.

Technology is rooted in the past.
It dominates the present and tends into the future.
It is a real historical movement—
one of the great movements which shape and
represent their epoch.
It can be compared only with the Classic
discovery of man as a person,
the Roman will to power,
and the religious movement of the Middle Ages.
Technology is far more than a method,
it is a world in itself.
As a method it is superior in almost every respect.
But only where it is left to itself as in
gigantic structures of engineering, there
technology reveals its true nature.
There it is evident that it is not only a useful means,
that it is something, something in itself,
something that has a meaning and a powerful form—
so powerful in fact, that it is not easy to name it.
Is that still technology or is it architecture?
And that may be the reason why some people
are convinced that architecture will be outmoded
and replaced by technology.
Such a conviction is not based on clear thinking.
The opposite happens.
Wherever technology reaches its real fulfillment,
it transcends into architecture.
It is true that architecture depends on facts,
but its real field of activity is in the realm
of significance.
I hope you will understand that architecture
has nothing to do with the inventions of forms.
It is not a playground for children, young or old.
Architecture is the real battleground of the spirit.
Architecture wrote the history of the epochs
and gave them their names.

Architecture depends on its time.
It is the crystallization of its inner structure,
the slow unfolding of its form.
That is the reason why technology and architecture
are so closely related.
Our real hope is that they grow together,
that someday the one be the expression of
the other.
Only then will we have an architecture worthy
of its name:
Architecture as a true symbol of our time.

LUDWIG MIES VAN DER ROHE
Address to the Illinois Institute of Technology, 1950

One of the most spectacular and successful exhibits at Expo '67 in Mon-
treal was Moshe Safdie's housing complex, Habitat. Although the Israeli-
born architect's hope that other structures similar to Habitat would
soon be built has not been fulfilled, Safdie believes important lessons for
the future of housing design were gained from the experience.

The design cost of Habitat, two million dollars, is building research. In
a way the whole cost of design and construction, twenty million dollars, should be considered research. Just as the car manufacturers
hand-make a test model so Habitat was a hand-made prototype of what
eventually could go on a mechanized assembly line. Habitat was more
hand-made than even a conventional building. We were following a
process of trial and error, trying things out and changing them in the
building. The contractor of Habitat estimated that whereas the
efficiency of a car assembly line is eighty per cent in terms of the
workers' productive time versus idle time, and the efficiency on the
average construction job is thirty to forty per cent, on Habitat it was
ten per cent.

I do not believe that careful pre-planning would have prevented
that amount of wasted time. Most of the time we were learning lessons,
not making mistakes. We were learning things that could not have been
predicted without physically doing them, for real, in full size. We were
stretching the existing state of the building art far beyond its accepted
capabilities. . . .

If we apply factory efficiencies to the construction industry, the
financial relationship between owner, designer, manufacturer, and contractor must also change, it has to be integrated, made into a single
entity. I see no way in which meaningful technical advances can be
made unless total integration takes place. You can't deal with thirty different labor unions on a single assembly line, yet that's what we were
trying to do in Habitat. The implications are clear: The obvious, even
if not the safest, North American solution is for the great corporations,

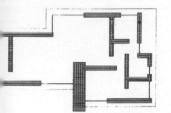

which are already involved in making everything from space ships to roasters, to start making the buildings.

If we could achieve this integration, the architect, who up to now has acted as an ivory-towered prima donna making sketches that the contractor will hopefully transform into a building, would become part of a much greater entity. Architects today are certainly resisting any such change. But I'm afraid they are going to be gradually pushed out of the picture. Today, architects in North America design only twenty per cent of all buildings. If they persist in their attitude this percentage will dwindle until only the odd museum and concert hall will be architect-designed. A new profession of industrial building designers will be created by the great corporations. . . .

Technology today means mass production, the assembly line, large-scale organization, corporate structure—whether it's in Russia or the United States. It means automation. It means integrated production. In the field of environment, it also means a tremendous threat to human identity and aspirations. Not only architects, but the public too, are terrified of it.

People recognize that our technology basically means doing things in great numbers, which means repetition, which implies the kind of organization that operates on centralized decisions. Nothing more powerfully symbolizes the conflict between the individual and a centralized, numerically-oriented process than the concern with environment. The fear is that the environment will become stereotyped, repetitive, monotonous, overwhelming—a place where the individual will feel that he has lost his identity or, even more serious, has lost control. People make the link between mass production and monotony, even further discouraging the industrialist from going into mass-produced housing. . . .

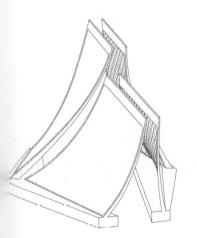

The challenge of today is to understand the problems our technology introduces in the environment . . . . Only an understanding of the issue can reduce the threat. And there is no use rejecting new technology in building; we have no choice, any more than we had a choice in industrializing agriculture. The only choice there, was between famine or plenty; the choice here is between a decent shelter or no shelter. Are we going to have an environment fit for human beings or mass dehumanization of environment leading to a regression of our species?

Habitat tries to show that it is possible to have an environment that is not monotonous, one that has the possibility of identity and of variety, choice and spatial richness, and yet at the same time the use of repetitive mass-produced systems. For me that is where Habitat has been most successful. The fact that the actual components in Habitat were hand-made is irrelevant in the face of the demonstration that a few repetitive components could be assembled to form a variety of houses and community spaces, the kind of environment that people normally associate with the non-industrialized, handcrafted, vernacular village.

People visiting Habitat were reminded of a Mediterranean village.

That association was not rooted in formalism; it is generic in nature. The typical Aegean hill villages, the Arab hill towns, or the Indian pueblos are true building systems. They consist of a vocabulary of repetitive components—for example, the Arab village with its cubical room, dome, vault, and court. These components are manipulated by the individual who builds his own house. The houses are grouped along alleys and streets in harmony with the site. Habitat is in the tradition of spontaneous self-made environments, the beginnings of a contemporary vernacular.

MOSHE SAFDIE
Beyond Habitat, 1970

Philip C. Johnson's career has been composed of equal parts of architectural design and criticism. In collaboration with Henry Russell Hitchcock, Johnson popularized the phrase "international style" to describe the architecture of the 1930's and wrote the standard critical treatment of the era. After the end of World War II Johnson earned a bachelor of architecture degree from Harvard and later became an associate of Mies van der Rohe—participating in the planning of the Seagram Building. Today Johnson's individual works, ranging from his unique home in Connecticut to the New York State Theater at Lincoln Center, are considered modern classics. With this varied background Johnson was well suited to the task of alerting students of architectural design at Harvard to some of the pitfalls of his profession.

I'm going to attack the seven crutches of architecture. Some of us rejoice in the crutches and pretend that we're walking and that poor other people with two feet are slightly handicapped. But we all use them at times, and especially in the schools where you have to use language. It's only natural to use language when you're teaching, because how are teachers to mark you? "Bad entrance" or "Bathrooms not backed up" or "Stairway too narrow" or "Where's head room?", "Chimney won't draw," "Kitchen too far from dining room." It is so much easier for the faculty to set up a set of rules that you can be marked against. They can't say "That's ugly." For you can answer that for you it is good-looking, and de gustibus non est disputandum. Schools therefore are especially prone to using these crutches. I would certainly use them if I were teaching, because I couldn't criticize extra-aesthetic props any better than any other teacher.

The most important crutch in recent times is not valid now: the Crutch of History. In the old days you could always rely on books. You could say, "What do you mean you don't like my tower? There it is in Wren." Or, "They did that on the Subtreasury Building—why can't I do it?" History doesn't bother us very much now.

But the next one is still with us today although, here again, the Crutch of Pretty Drawing is pretty well gone. There are those of us—I

am one—who have made sort of a cult of the pretty plan. It's a wonderful crutch because you can give yourself the illusion that you are creating architecture while you're making pretty drawings. Fundamentally, architecture is something you build and put together, and people walk in and they like it. But that's too hard. Pretty pictures are easier.

The next one, the third one, is the Crutch of Utility, of Usefulness. This is where I was brought up, and I've used it myself; it was an old Harvard habit. They say a building is good architecture if it works. Of course, this is poppycock. All buildings work. This building (referring to Hunt Hall) works perfectly—if I talk loud enough. The Parthenon probably worked perfectly well for the ceremonies that they used it for. In other words, merely that a building works is not sufficient. You expect that it works. You expect a kitchen hot water faucet to run hot water these days. You expect any architect, a graduate of Harvard or not, to be able to put the kitchen in the right place. But when it's used as a crutch it impedes. It lulls you into thinking that that is architecture. The rules that we've all been brought up on "The coat closet should be near the front door in a house," "Cross-ventilation is a necessity,"—these rules are not very important for architecture. That we should have a front door to come in and a back door to carry the garbage out—pretty good, but in my house I noticed to my horror the other day that I carried the garbage out the front door. If the business of getting the house to run well takes precedence over your artistic invention the result won't be architecture at all; merely an assemblage of useful parts. You will recognize it next time you're doing a building: you'll be so satisfied when you get the banks of elevators to come out at the right floor you'll think your skyscraper is finished. I know. I'm just working on one.

That's not as bad, though, as the next one: the Crutch of Comfort. That's a habit that we come by, the same as utility. We are all descended from John Stuart Mill in our thinking. After all, what is architecture for but the comforts of the people that live there? But when that is made into a crutch for doing architecture, environmental control starts to replace architecture. Pretty soon you'll be doing controlled environmental houses which aren't hard to do except that you may have a window on the west and you can't control the sun. There isn't an overhang in the world, there isn't a sun chart in Harvard University that will help. Because, of course, the sun is absolutely everywhere. You know what they mean by controlled environment—it is the study of "microclimatology," which is the science that tells you how to recreate a climate so that you will be comfortable. But are you? The fireplace, for example, is out of place in the controlled environment of a house. It heats up and throws off thermostats. But I like the beauty of a fireplace so I keep my thermostat way down to 60, and then I light a big roaring fire. . . . Now that's not controlled environment. I control the environment. It's a lot more fun.

Some people say that chairs are good-looking that are comfortable. Are they? I think that comfort is a function of whether you think the chair is good-looking or not. Just test it yourself. (Except I know you won't be honest with me.) I have had Mies van der Rohe chairs now for twenty-five years in my home wherever I go. They're not very comfortable chairs, but, if people like the looks of them they say "Aren't these beautiful chairs," which indeed they are. Then they'll sit in them and say, "My, aren't they comfortable." If, however, they're the kind of people who think curving steel legs are an ugly way to hold up a chair they'll say "My, what uncomfortable chairs."

The Crutch of Cheapness. That is one that you haven't run into as students because no one's told you to cut $10,000 off the budget because you haven't built anything. But that'll be your first lesson. The cheapness boys will say "Anybody can build an expensive house. Ah, but see, my house only cost $25,000." Anybody that can build a $25,000 house has indeed reason to be proud, but is he talking about architecture or his economic ability? Is it the crutch you're talking about, or is it architecture? That economic motive, for instance, goes in New York so far that the real estate minded people consider it un-American to build a Lever House with no rentals on the ground floor. They find that it's an architectural sin not to fill the envelope.

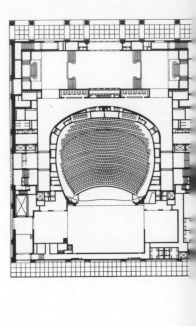

Then there's another very bad crutch that you will get much later in your career. Please, please watch out for this one: the Crutch of Serving the Client. You can escape all criticism if you can say, "Well, the client wanted it that way." Mr. Hood, one of our really great architects, talked exactly that way. He would put a Gothic door on a skyscraper and say "Why shouldn't I? The client wanted a Gothic door on the modern skyscraper, and I put it on. Because what is my business? Am I not here to please my client?" As one of the boys asked me during the dinner before the lecture, where do you draw the line? When do the client's demands permit you to shoot him, and when do you give in gracefully? It's got to be clear, back in your own mind, that serving the client is one thing and the art of architecture another.

Perhaps the most trouble of all is the Crutch of Structure. That gets awfully near home because, of course, I use it all the time myself. I'm going to go on using it. You have to use something. Like Bucky Fuller, who's going around from school to school—it's like a hurricane, you can't miss it if it's coming: he talks, you know, for five or six hours, and he ends up that all architecture is nonsense, and you have to build something like discontinuous domes. The arguments are beautiful. I have nothing against discontinuous domes, but for goodness sakes, let's not call it architecture. Have you ever seen Bucky trying to put a door into one of his domed buildings? He's never succeeded, and wisely, when he does them, he doesn't put any covering on them, so they are magnificent pieces of pure sculpture. Sculpture alone cannot result in architecture because architecture has problems that Bucky Fuller has not faced, like how do you get in and out. Structure is a very danger-

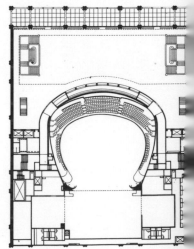

ous thing to cling to. You can be led to believe that clear structure clearly expressed will end up being architecture by itself. You say, "I don't have to design any more. All I have to do is make a clean structural order." I have believed this off and on myself. It's a very nice crutch, you see, because, after all, you can't mess up a building too badly if the bays are all equal and all the windows the same size.

Now why should we at this stage be that crutch conscious? Why should we not step right up to it and face it? The act of creation. The act of creation, like birth and death, you have to face by yourself. There aren't any rules; there is no one to tell you whether your one choice out of, say, six billion for the proportion of a window is going to be right. No one can go with you into that room where you make the final decision. You can't escape it anyhow; why fight it? Why not realize that architecture is the sum of inescapable artistic decisions that you have to make. If you're strong you can make them.

I like the thought that what we are to do on this earth is to embellish it for its greater beauty, so that oncoming generations can look back to the shapes we leave here and get the same thrill that I get in looking back at theirs—at the Parthenon, at Chartres Cathedral. That is the duty—I doubt if I get around to it in my generation—the difficulties are too many, but you can. You can if you're strong enough not to bother with the crutches, and face the fact that to create something is a direct experience.

I like Corbusier's definition of architecture. He expressed it the way I wish I could have: "L'architecture, c'est le jeux, savant, correct et magnifique, des formes sous la lumière"—"Architecture is the play of forms under the light, the play of forms correct, wise, magnificent." The play of forms under the light. And, my friends, that's all it is. You can embellish architecture by putting toilets in. But there was great architecture long before the toilet was invented. I like Nietzsche's definition—that much-misunderstood European—he said, "In architectural works, man's pride, man's triumph over gravitation, man's will to power assume visible form. Architecture is a veritable oratory of power made by form."

PHILIP C. JOHNSON
Remarks at Harvard College, 1954

A Chronology of Architecture

Man leaves caves and begins to build huts and other rough shelters	c.8000 B.C.	The last ice sheets recede, marking the end of the Pleistocene Period and the beginning of the Mesolithic Period; the ice retreat opens up vast, new regions for settlement
Dolmens, megaliths that today are freestanding but were once part of earthen mounds containing upright and lintel stones, make their appearance; menhirs, isolated stone monoliths, also date from this period	5000	Neolithic Period; man ceases being a nomad and settles in one place, growing his own food
The White Temple of Warka is built; its base is the earliest form of the Babylonian ziggurat	3200-2850	Sumerian city-states dominated by temple complexes emerge in Lower Mesopotamia; writing is invented
Egyptian tombs of the mastaba type, rectangular structures with flat roofs, are constructed	3000	Menes unites Upper and Lower Egypt and proclaims the First Dynasty; writing and the hieroglyphic system develop
Step Pyramid of Zoser, world's first large-scale monument in stone, is built at Sakkara	2778	Beginning of Egypt's Third Dynasty
Great Pyramid constructed by Cheops at Giza; Chephren erects a second pyramid and the Sphinx at Giza; Mycerinus builds third and last pyramid	2723-2563	Fourth Dynasty; zenith of Egypt's Old Kingdom
Palace of King Minos is constructed in Knossos; the civic center is destroyed in 1400	1728-1686 1600	Reign of Hammurabi marks Babylon's golden age
Mortuary Temple of Hatshepsut is built at Thebes	1580-332 1520	Egypt's New Kingdom
	1400-1200	Period of Mycenaean ascendancy; it is ended by the Trojan War
	1100-800	Greece is enveloped in a dark age
	650-323	Hellenic period in Greece; rise of city-states; the Age of Pericles (444-29) marks the climax of a period of intense intellectual ferment and a flowering of the arts
Nebuchadnezzar II rebuilds Babylon; Hanging Gardens and Ishtar Gate constructed	605-563	
	509	Traditional date of the founding of the Roman Republic
The Parthenon, the supreme achievement of Greek architecture, is erected on the Athens Acropolis	447-38	
Temple of Athena Nike added to Acropolis	427-25	
The Erechtheum built on the Acropolis	421-06	
Great Stupa begun at Sanchi; it is characteristic of non-Mogul Indian architecture	300	
The Romans begin work on the Via Appia, uniting Rome with the south of Italy; construction of Rome's first aqueduct is also begun	312	
Great Wall of China completed	214	
	146	Greece becomes a Roman province
Romans build Sanctuary of Fortuna Primigenia at Palestrina	82-79	
	60	Caesar, Crassus, and Pompey form Rome's First Triumvirate
Julius Caesar builds a new, larger forum in Rome, establishing a precedent that will be followed by Emperors Augustus, Vespasian, Nerva, and Trajan	54	
	44	Julius Caesar assassinated
	30	Egypt becomes a province of Rome
Augustus launches extensive building programs in Rome, transforming it from a city of bricks to a city of marble	27 B.C.-A.D. 14	Reign of Augustus Caesar, Rome's first emperor; he initiates the Pax Romana, a 200-year period of peace
Agrippa erects a temple that is the precursor of the Pantheon; it is severely damaged by fire in the first century A.D.	25 B.C.	
Theater of Marcellus completed in Rome; a different Greek order of columns is used for each of its tiers, a convention in later Roman theater and amphitheater building	11	

Hagia Sophia is looted and damaged during sack of Constantinople by Crusaders	1204	
Reims Cathedral is built	1211-90	
	1215	Magna Carta signed by King John at Runnymede
	1271-95	Marco Polo journeys to the Orient
Construction of Cologne Cathedral, the largest Gothic church in Northern Europe, is begun	1248	
	1337	Outbreak of the Hundred Years' War
	1368	Founding of the Ming dynasty in China
	1415	Battle of Agincourt; English forces under Henry V defeat the French in a climactic battle of the Hundred Years' War
Brunelleschi's dome caps the Florence Duomo; triumphant blend of a Renaissance dome with a Gothic building	1420-34	
Foundling Hospital constructed in Florence; Brunelleschi's building is first in the Renaissance style	1421-45	
Pazzi Chapel, also by Brunelleschi, built in Florence	1429-46	
Leon Battista Alberti's Palazzo Rucellai in Florence exhibits the tiers of pilasters that become a major style of the Renaissance	1446-51	
	1453	Fall of Constantinople to the Ottoman Turks
	1492	Fall of Granada marks the end of Islamic influence in Spain; Christopher Columbus makes first of four voyages to the New World
Bramante's Tempietto, one of the finest examples of High Renaissance, constructed in Rome	1502-10	
St. Peter's Basilica erected in Rome; it owes its spectacular dome to Michelangelo	1506-1626	
	1508	Michelangelo begins painting the ceiling of the Sistine Chapel
	1516	Martin Luther posts his ninety-five theses
Michelangelo's Medici Chapel rises in Florence	1519-21	Magellan circumnavigates the globe
Rome's Farnese Palace is designed by Antonio da Sangallo the Younger; Michelangelo adds a third story to the building in 1546	1521-34 1530	
	1534	Act of Supremacy names Henry VIII head of the Church of England
	1543	Copernicus publishes his discoveries on the nature of the solar system
Jacopo Sansovino's Library of St. Mark is built in Venice	1536-53	
The Louvre is built in Paris; it manifests a complete history of the French Renaissance	1546-1878	
El Escorial exemplifies the Renaissance in Spain	1559-84	
Andrea Palladio, the most influential architect of the Renaissance, publishes *The Four Books of Architecture*; the designs in his book, rather than his buildings, influence architects throughout Europe	1570	
	1588	England turns back the Spanish Armada; Christopher Marlowe's *Dr. Faustus* performed
Inigo Jones's Banqueting House manifests the influence of Palladio in England	1601 1619-22	First performance of Shakespeare's *Hamlet*
The Taj Mahal, Mogul India's greatest monument, is built at Agra	1620 1630-53	Pilgrims land at Plymouth Rock, Massachusetts
	1632	Galileo publishes his work supporting Copernicus's theories on the solar system; the following year he is tried for heresy by the Inquisition
Louis XIV commences the building of Versailles; the magnificent palace involved enormous expenditures in money and labor and represents the height of the French Neoclassical style	1661	
Christopher Wren's masterpiece, St. Paul's replaces an earlier cathedral destroyed in the Great Fire	1666 1675-1710	Great Fire of London virtually destroys the city

During Venetian siege of Athens, the Parthenon is badly damaged	1687	
	1688	Glorious Revolution in England
Schoenbrunn, the Habsburg imperial residence that is modeled on Versailles, is constructed in Vienna	1696-1700	
Blenheim Palace, the most monumental mansion in England, is built in the Baroque style	1705-20	
	1710	Berkeley's *Treatise concerning the Principles of Human Knowledge* inaugurates empiricism
	1713	Treaty of Utrecht
	1740	War of the Austrian Succession embroils Europe in a major war
The Petit Trianon is constructed at Versailles; intimate in scale, graceful in proportions, it exemplifies the Classical revival	1762-68	
	1776	American Declaration of Independence; James Watt invents the steam engine; Adam Smith publishes *The Wealth of Nations*
The iron bridge at Coalbrookdale in Britain is the first of its kind	1779	
	1789	Parisians storm the Bastille; Declaration of the Rights of Man proclaimed
James Hoban designs the President's House, for Washington, D.C., in the English Palladian style	1792	
	1803	United States purchases Louisiana Territory
	1804	Napoleon proclaimed emperor of France
The Madelaine, a copy of a Greek peripteral temple, is constructed in Paris	1806-42	
	1812-14	The War of 1812; British burn Washington, D.C.
	1815	Napoleon defeated at Waterloo
John Nash's Royal Pavilion constructed at Brighton; it is an early example of Eclecticism	1815-21	
United States Capitol, originally planned on Palladian lines by William Thornton, is rebuilt by Latrobe and Bullfinch after the War of 1812	1815-29	
The mammoth British Museum, Greek Revival in style, is built by Robert Smirke	1823-47	
	1824	First trade union formed in England
	1837	Accession of Queen Victoria of England
The Houses of Parliament in London exemplify the Gothic revival	1840-60	
	1848	Revolutionary movements erupt and are quelled in Germany, Italy, Austria; abdication of Louis Philippe and proclamation of the Second Republic; Marx and Engels publish *Communist Manifesto*
John Ruskin, a proponent of the Gothic revival, publishes *The Seven Lamps of Architecture*	1849	
Crystal Palace erected in Hyde Park to house the Great Exhibition; its iron framework is exposed	1850-51	
	1854	Commodore Perry opens Japan to Western trade
Elisha Graves Otis installs first safety passenger elevator in a department store in New York	1857	
	1859	Charles Darwin publishes *Origin of Species* . . .
	1861-65	The American Civil War
	1874	First major exhibit of Impressionist paintings held in Paris
H. H. Richardson builds the Marshall Field Wholesale Warehouse in Chicago; it has a strong influence on later skyscraper building	1885-87	
Dankmar Adler and Louis Sullivan build the Auditorium Building in Chicago	1886-89	
The Reliance Building is constructed in Chicago	1890	
	1895	Publication of Freud's *Studies on Hysteria* marks the beginning of psychoanalysis
Louis Sullivan's most notable work, the Schlesinger-Mayer Store (today Carson, Pirie, Scott and Co.), is erected in Chicago	1899-1904	
	1903	Wright brothers design first airplane

Antoni Gaudí builds the Casa Milá in Barcelona	1905-10	
	1905-16	Albert Einstein formulates special and general theories of relativity
	1907	Exhibition of Pablo Picasso's *Les Demoiselles d'Avignon* marks beginning of Cubism
New York's Woolworth Building marks an important advance in skyscraper building	1911-13	
Walter Gropius founds the Bauhaus	1919	Treaty of Versailles ends World War I
Le Corbusier builds the most famous of his many houses, Villa Les Terraces at Garches, near Paris	1926-27	
	1928	Discovery of penicillin by Alexander Fleming
	1929	Stock market crash on Wall Street leads to worldwide economic depression
Empire State Building erected in New York; it remains world's tallest skyscraper for forty years	1930-32	
Rockefeller Center complex constructed	1931-39	
Philadelphia Savings Fund Society Building opens; first American building in the steel-and-glass form	1932	
The Nazis close the Bauhaus	1933	Adolf Hitler becomes chancellor of Germany
	1936	Spanish Civil War begins
Frank Lloyd Wright builds Falling Water, a private home that exemplifies architecture as an extension of the environment	1936-37	
Frank Lloyd Wright's Johnson Wax Company factory complex is built in Racine, Wisconsin	1936-49	
	1939	German invasion of Poland marks beginning of World War II
	1945	Allies defeat Hitler's Germany; first atomic bombs used against Japan to end World War II in the Pacific; United Nations organized
Le Corbusier constructs Unités d'Habitation in Marseille; designed to house a complete community, it illustrates his plan for a "vertical city"	1946-52	
United Nations Headquarters is erected in New York City under an international team of architects that includes Le Corbusier, Wallace Harrison, Oscar Niemeyer and Sven Markelius	1947-53	
	1948	State of Israel established
Pier Luigi Nervi's remarkable Exhibition Hall in Turin, Italy, is completed in only eight months	1948-49	
	1949	People's Republic of China proclaimed
	1950-52	Korean War
Lever House opens on New York's Park Avenue	1952	
Chandigarh, the new administration capital of India's Punjab state that was designed by Le Corbusier, is inaugurated	1953	
Nervi builds the Palazzetto dello Sport in Rome	1956-57	
	1957	Sputnik I launched by Soviet Union
Mies van der Rohe's Seagram Building completed	1958	Charles de Gaulle elected president of France; establishment of the Fifth Republic
The Solomon R. Guggenheim Museum, by Frank Lloyd Wright, opens in New York	1959	
Eero Saarinen's Trans World Airlines Terminal at J.F.K. International Airport in New York is built	1962	Cuban missile crisis
Lincoln Center for the Performing Arts is constructed in New York	1962-68	
	1963	Assassination of President John F. Kennedy
World Trade Center proposed in New York City; its twin 1,350-foot towers are scheduled for completion in 1975	1964	Civil Rights Act passed by U.S. Congress
Eero Saarinen's CBS Building adds a granite sheath to the familiar glass-and-steel skyscraper form	1965	
Habitat, Moshe Safdie's experimental housing complex, is built for Expo '67 in Montreal	1967	Arab-Israeli Six-Day War; first heart transplant performed by Dr. Christiaan Barnard
	1969	American astronauts walk on the moon
The Sidney Opera House opens; Sears Tower, world's tallest building, opens in Chicago	1973	Agreement signed to end the Vietnam War

Selected Bibliography

Anderson, W. J., Ashby, T., and Spiers, R. P. *The Architecture of Greece and Rome*. New York: Charles Scribner's Sons, 1922.

Branner, R. *Gothic Architecture*. New York: George Braziller, 1961.

Burchard, J. and Bush-Brow, A. *The Architecture of America*. Boston: Atlantic-Little, Brown and Co., 1961.

Cook, J. W. and Klotz, H. *Conversations with Architects*. New York: Praeger Publishers, 1973.

Corfiato, H. O. and Richardson, A. *The Art of Architecture*. New York: Philosophical Library Inc., 1956.

Fletcher, B. *A History of Architecture on the Comparative Method*. (Seventeenth edition.) New York: Charles Scribner's Sons, 1967.

Giedion, S. *Space, Time and Architecture*. (Fifth edition.) Cambridge, Mass.: Harvard University Press, 1967.

Gropius, W. *The New Architecture and the Bauhaus*. London: Faber & Faber, Ltd., 1935.

Hamlin, T. *Architecture Through the Ages*. (Second edition, revised.) New York: G. P. Putnam's Sons, 1953.

Hitchcock, H. R. *Architecture, Nineteenth and Twentieth Centuries*. Harmondsworth: Penguin Books Ltd., 1958.

Hitchcock, H. R. and Johnson, P. *The International Style*. New York: W. W. Norton, 1932.

Huxtable, A.L. *Pier Luigi Nervi*. New York: George Braziller, 1960.

———. *Will They Ever Finish Bruckner Boulevard?* New York: Macmillan, 1970.

Kidson, P., Murray, P., and Thompson, P. *A History of English Architecture*. Harmondsworth: Penguin Books Ltd., 1965.

Le Corbusier. *Towards a New Architecture*. New York: Payson & Clarke, Ltd., 1927.

Lowry, B. *Renaissance Architecture*. New York: George Braziller, 1962.

Mâle, E. *The Gothic Image*. New York: Harper & Row, 1973.

Mumford, L. *The Culture of the Cities*. New York: Harcourt, Brace & World, 1938.

Pevsner, N. *An Outline of European Architecture*. Harmondsworth: Penguin Books Ltd., 1960.

———. *Pioneers of Modern Design*. Harmondsworth: Penguin Books Ltd., 1960.

Ruskin, J. *The Seven Lamps of Architecture*. New York: E. P. Dutton, Inc., 1956.

Scully, V. J. *Modern Architecture*. New York: George Braziller, 1961.

Sullivan, L. H. *The Autobiography of an Idea*. New York: American Institute of Architects Press, 1924.

Venturi, R. *Complexity and Contradiction in Architecture*. New York: Museum of Modern Art, 1966.

Viollet-le-duc, E. *Discourses on Architecture*. New York: Grove Press, 1959.

Webb, G. *Architecture in Britain—The Middle Ages*. Harmondsworth: Penguin Books Ltd., 1958.

Wittkower, R. *Art and Architecture in Italy; 1600–1750*. Harmondsworth: Penguin Books Ltd., 1958.

Wright, F. L. *Modern Architecture*. Princeton, N.J.: Princeton University Press, 1931.

Picture Credits

HALFTITLE Symbol designed by Jay J. Smith Studio FRONTISPIECE (Cirani)

CHAPTER 1 **6** (Ciol) **8** (A.C.L., Brussels) Diagrams: Damascus Museum **9** (Aerofilms, Ltd. London) **10** (AME) **11** (Begotti) **12–13** (Kodansha) **14** left (AME); right (Bildarchiv Photo Marburg); bottom (CEAM) **15** left (Arborio Mella); center (Anderson); right (Balestrini) **16** (Cirani) **17** (Favole)

CHAPTER 2 **18** (Kodansha) **20** (Hamlyn Picture Library) **21** (Hamlyn Picture Library) **22–23** (Cirani) **24** (Bildarchiv Photo Marburg) **24–25** (Arborio

Index